PHIL JACKSON

JOHN FREDRIC EVANS

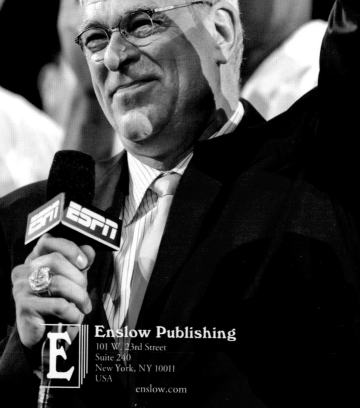

Enslow Publishing
101 W. 23rd Street
Suite 240
New York, NY 10011
USA

enslow.com

Published in 2020 by Enslow Publishing, LLC
101 W. 23rd Street, Suite 240, New York, NY 10011

Library of Congress Cataloging-in-Publication Data

Names: Evans, John Fredric, author.
Title: Phil Jackson / John Fredric Evans.
Description: New York : Enslow Publishing LLC, 2020. | Series: Championship Coaches | Includes bibliographical references and index. | Audience: Grades: 7-12.
Identifiers: LCCN 2018002103| ISBN 9780766097971 (library bound) | ISBN 9780766097988 (paperback)
Subjects: LCSH: Jackson, Phil—Juvenile literature. | Basketball coaches—United States—Biography—Juvenile literature. | Chicago Bulls (Basketball team)—History—Juvenile literature. | Los Angeles Lakers (Basketball team)—History—Juvenile literature.
Classification: LCC GV884.J32 E83 2019 | DDC 796.323092 [B] —dc23
LC record available at https://lccn.loc.gov/2018002103

Printed in China

To Our Readers: We have done our best to make sure all website addresses in this book were active and appropriate when we went to press. However, the author and the publisher have no control over and assume no liability for the material available on those websites or on any websites they may link to. Any comments or suggestions can be sent by email to customerservice@enslow.com.

Photo Credits: Cover, p. 1, Paul J. Richards/AFP/Getty Images; pp. 7, 12, 16, 27, 34, 43, 49, 50, 66, 79, 82, 92 © AP Images; p. 8 Collegiate Images/Getty Images; pp. 18, 23, 37, 61 Focus on Sport/Getty Images; p. 20 New York Daily News Archive/Getty Images; p. 29 Icon Sportswire/Getty Images; p. 38 Al Seib/Los Angeles Times/Getty Images; p. 40 Tom Berg/WireImage/Getty Images; p. 58 Tommaso Boddi/WireImage/Getty Images; p. 68 Brian Bahr/AFP/Getty Images; p. 72 Jeff Haynes/AFP/Getty Images; p. 91 Ronald Martinez/Getty Images; p. 94 Maddie Meyer/Getty Images.

CONTENTS

INTRODUCTION

The "Zen Master." Phil Jackson's nickname may carry a tinge of sarcasm, but it does reflect his unique identity. Despite being the most untraditional of sports coaches, Jackson has won more National Basketball Association championships (eleven) than anyone in his position. In fact, no coach in any of the major professional sports has come close, other than hockey's Scotty Bowman (nine NHL titles). A Phil Jackson team has never missed the playoffs. His career winning percentage tops that of any other NBA coach in the Basketball Hall of Fame. Coaching Michael Jordan and Kobe Bryant sure didn't hurt, but plenty of other coaches didn't win titles with those guys.

Most great leaders are aware that winning teams must play in selfless harmony. Jackson has his own methods of creating this collective consciousness. He built his offense around the Triangle system because it asks a team to share the ball, which for Jackson is a metaphor for meaningful collaboration. "Once the players have mastered the system, a powerful group intelligence emerges that is greater than the coach's ideas or those of any individual on the team,"[1] he's said.

Though Jackson is not a "rah-rah," "win one for the Gipper!" pep-talk giver, he presented his players in Chicago and Los Angeles with a comforting, paternal presence in the one-on-one meetings he made sure to arrange. Jud Buechler, a minimum-salary "twelfth man" on the Chicago Bulls, was blown away that his new coach not only asked him how his wife was settling in, but even knew her name. Jackson wanted everyone on the team to know they were important to him. "Over the years, I've learned to listen closely to players—not just what they say, but also their body language and the silence between the words,"[2] said Jackson. At the same time, his always-authentic approach has made him seem understated, even enigmatic. "My style is to show appreciation with subtle gestures—a nod of recognition here, a touch on the arm there,"[3] he said.

Jackson biographer Peter Richmond believes his subject is a seeker and a student as much as he is a teacher. "He never stopped questioning what's real and what counts in this very short lifetime. Native American culture, Buddhism, Christianity, mysticism—he kept exploring and he kept questioning."[4] This search for wisdom and mental strength has informed his coaching style with concepts seldom seen in sports or business. And yet, his unconventional approach has produced unprecedented success. Jackson's six championships with the Chicago Bulls and five with the Los Angeles Lakers will be difficult to duplicate.

Diane Mast, wife of a former teammate and a long-time friend of Jackson's, had this to say about Phil: "I've never known him as somebody, and then he became somebody else. He was always Phil. He still is Phil … a true good man, un-divine and imperfect, but good."[5]

And, of course, he's one heck of a coach.

1

THE JOURNEY BEGINS

- - - - - - - - - - - - - - - -

Charles and Elisabeth Jackson were both ministers in the Pentecostal movement, spreading the gospel in Montana, when Elisabeth gave birth to her third son, Phil Douglas Jackson, in 1945. She had captained her girls' basketball team, so perhaps it was no surprise that Phil gravitated to the game. His fifth-grade coach taught him the hook shot, which would remain his best offensive weapon.

Phil's parents were extremely strict, allowing no comic books, television, dancing, or moviegoing. Classmates teasingly called Phil and his siblings "holy rollers." As Phil remembers, "After a couple years of devoted prayer and supplication, I decided that this wasn't going to be my thing. I started desperately searching for school activities that would take me away from my nearly 24–7 life at church."[1] Nonetheless, his upbringing began Phil's lifelong quest for spiritual enlightenment.

Growing up in rural Montana, Phil was outdoorsy and athletic. Swimming, hockey, football, fishing and of course, basketball, kept him busy. "I suddenly realized that there could be a whole life for me away from home. Up to this time I'd had absolutely no exposure to the outside world, and I

> *"I think my carriage and my demeanor are very much what the image of my father was like."*[2]
> —Phil Jackson

subsequently jumped at every opportunity to get out and play ball."[3]

By seventh grade, basketball was his favorite game. "I don't think I was a particularly gifted athlete, it was just that I was good under stress, understood gamesmanship, and *loved* competition."[4] Despite the placid demeanor he became famous for, Phil was (and is) a fierce competitor.

As a shy kid, he believed that he'd earn acceptance by being the best at whatever he did. "Being liked socially was a way out of the triangle of family, school and church,"[5] he wrote in his 1975 book *Maverick*. Phil longed to escape the limitations of life in his parents' loving but tightly regulated household.

As a boy, Phil also became fascinated with the region's Native American traditions. He dreamt of living there a century earlier, in tune with nature before

Native American tribes thrived in Montana before European settlers arrived in the 1800s. In this 1958 photo, the Blackfoot's Isabelle Old Chief and her daughter Isabelle prepare lunch inside their teepee in East Glacier, Montana.

the coming of the white man. His reverence for Native American spiritual practices would continue to inform his beliefs for years to come.

The family made several moves around Montana before crossing state lines to settle in the town of Williston, North Dakota, when Phil was in eighth grade. After a ten-inch growth spurt during his freshman and sophomore years, Phil was saddled with the first of many nicknames, "Bones," because at six foot one (185 centimeters) and 150 pounds (68 kilograms), he was a tower of skin and bones. He was so self-conscious about his body that he never went swimming without a T-shirt.

On the court, Phil began to study and master the game in a way that few young players do. He soon understood the nuances of offense, grasping the logic behind screen-setting and cuts to the basket. He also learned how to counteract the movements of a defender. "What I liked about basketball was how interconnected everything was," said Phil. "The game was a complex dance of moves and countermoves that made it much more alive than other sports I played. In addition, basketball demanded a high level of synergy. To succeed, you needed to rely upon everybody else on the floor, not just yourself. That gave the sport a certain transcendent beauty I found deeply satisfying."[6]

As a college player, Jackson used his unusually long limbs to full advantage. He also became a prolific scorer.

His short-range hook shot was very hard to stop. He also saw that relying on jump shots, as his team often did, made it harder to score than an offense designed to get layups and create post-up opportunities near the basket. These observations would lead him to adopt the famed Triangle offense, years later.

One thing Phil's high school coach taught him was to tailor the game plan to suit the strength of his players. Firing on all cylinders, the squad reached the final game of the state tournament when Phil was a junior, and he scored twenty-seven points in a losing effort. By his senior year, Phil was six foot six (198 cm) and 180 pounds (82 kg). Not only could he block shots and rebound, he could dunk the ball. After scoring thirty-five points and being named MVP in the first state championship game ever televised throughout the state, Phil was the only player with the presence of mind, after the game, to thank the team's coaches, parents, and fans for their support.

A LARGER WORLD THAN BIG SKY COUNTRY

Though North Dakota wasn't a heavily scouted hotbed of athletic prospects, Phil did have options

A Sad History

A number of Native American tribes once lived on the lands we now call Montana, the most famous of them being the Cheyenne, Crow, Lakota, Shoshone, and Sioux. Native peoples occupied the land thousands of years before the first European explorers arrived in the early 1800s. Settlers brought with them epidemic diseases the natives had not developed a resistance to, resulting in many deaths due to illness. Tribes also suffered under the oppression of enslavement and forced labor. Today there are just seven federally recognized tribes left in Montana.

when it came to choosing his college. He was dismayed by the rather sleazy inducements of other schools and decided to attend the University of North Dakota, largely because the integrity of Fighting Sioux Coach Bill Fitch impressed him. Fitch declared there would be no illegal handouts or phony jobs to slip money to his players. He was also a warm and witty guy, which didn't hurt.

Phil registered for pre-law classes but soon changed course, instead studying psychology, philosophy, and religion. Darwin's theory of evolution was mind-blowing to him, and he studied a wide range of spiritual approaches spanning both Eastern and Western religions. "My head was swimming with ideas that challenged my core beliefs,"[8] Phil said of the conflict between his sheltered upbringing and university education.

> "You could correct [Phil], and you only had to do it once."[7]
>
> —Bill Fitch

As a seventeen-year-old freshman, Jackson was ineligible to play sports, and this gave him time to enjoy his newfound intellectual freedom. At North Dakota he studied religious mysticism, read the works of Plato and Nietzsche, and became fascinated by existentialists Camus, Sartre, Heidegger, and Jaspers. He was committed to discovering spiritual practices that felt right for him.

Once he got to compete in college sports, as a sophomore, Jackson was initially better at baseball than basketball. As a pitcher, he threw a tricky curve ball. But, as his basketball coach would later say, "Phil couldn't find home plate with a Geiger counter."[9]

While Jackson's long limbs may have hurt his accuracy from the mound, on the court that large wingspan made him a natural fit in a pressing defense. The press tries to deny the other team the simplest acts of inbounding the ball and moving it down the floor. Jackson's arms were so long, in fact, that he could sit in the backseat of a car and open both the driver's door and front passenger's door without even leaning forward.

A tendency to hit the hardwood chasing loose balls earned Jackson another nickname: "Mop." Fitch appreciated what a hard worker the kid was. Jackson's willingness to listen to, retain, and implement coaching was impressive. "You could correct him, and you only had to do it once … That was the result of being raised by two great parents,"[10] said the Sioux coach.

In Fitch's intelligent brand of offense, which kept the ball moving through principles of the Triangle, Jackson developed into a dominant post presence, often scoring at will with his signature hook shot and back-to-the-basket moves. He averaged more than twenty-seven points per game, topped fifty twice, and became a team leader. "The season may have seemed like a great personal

Fitch Could Fix It

A former drill sergeant in the US Marines, Bill Fitch certainly knew how to instill discipline in his teams. Coaching in the NBA, he became known as a turnaround artist who could take over struggling teams and mold them into winners. The NBA Coach of the Year Award tends to honor coaches who produced surprising results with an unexpectedly good team, and Fitch won it twice (once more than Phil Jackson). In 1979–80, he took over a 29–53 Boston Celtics team and led them to a 61–21 mark before winning an NBA championship the following year.

Jackson's coach at North Dakota, Bill Fitch, used an offensive system not unlike the Triangle. He soon went on to the NBA. In this 1971 photo, Fitch (*far right*) is the Cleveland Cavaliers' coach.

success for me," Jackson said later. "But more than accumulating impressive numbers, my experience that year revolved around the importance of staying focused on team goals, of not giving up on my teammates, of showing them the way on and off the court."[11]

At the NCAA Small College Tournament, the team made it to the Final Four for the second year in a row but lost to Louisiana Tech with two NBA scouts in the stands: Red Holzman and Jerry Krause. After getting in early foul trouble Jackson would play only twenty minutes, but both scouts coveted the talented forward, and both would figure heavily into his future career.

With the fifth selection in the second round of the 1967 NBA Draft, Holzman's New York Knicks selected Phil Jackson. The Knicks' scout had said "eh" when Krause asked what he thought of Jackson, so Krause believed Jackson would be there when his own team picked. No such luck. Back then, a second round pick would make $13,500—equivalent to nearly $100,000 today—but Jackson wasn't convinced by the money. He told Holzman he was having second thoughts about professional basketball. His original plan had been to attend graduate school and become a minister. Holzman assured Jackson that he would still be plenty young enough to pursue another career when his playing days were over, and Jackson signed his one-year contract. In *Maverick,* he explained this decision by saying, "I was a little frightened about going to New York, but I expected that the adventure might help me locate the center of my soul."[12]

The rough-and-tumble streets of New York in the late 1960s were a far cry from the Great Plains, and at first Jackson experienced culture shock. After Holzman picked him up at the airport, teenagers threw a big rock at the car and shattered the windshield. Though he was outraged, Holzman just kept driving. "Welcome to New York City," he told Jackson. "If you can take that, you'll do just fine here."[13]

Not only would Jackson be "fine" in the big city, he would thrive there.

2

THE PURITY OF UNSELFISH PLAY

- - - - - - - - - - - - - - - - - - -

While Jackson found the Big Apple's diversity and vital energy invigorating, he was alarmed by the hostility he saw between people on the streets and the subway, where he was once threatened with a knife. "I was shocked at how everybody's hostility seemed close to the surface,"[1] he said. This incivility extended to Knicks games, where brawls were commonplace, and Jackson would find himself drawn into more than one. He adapted quickly.

There was great talent on the Knicks, and when Holzman took over as coach, they discovered discipline and teamwork. Red's unselfish offensive philosophy would soon become Jackson's as well: move the ball and hit the open man. To play for Holzman, you had to be willing to sacrifice your own shot if a teammate had a better one. Defensively, they often went to the full-court press, which Jackson was very comfortable with. With the wingspan of a seven-footer, his quick hands and knack for deflecting passes, he could really disrupt an offense. The forward's insertion into a game was an injection of chaos. "When Phil came in, you absolutely knew that something was going to happen," said teammate Jerry Lucas. "He might steal a ball four times in a row, or foul out in fifty seconds. Of course, he was a good teammate, obviously; selfishness did not exist on that team."[2]

"Looking back at my playing career, it's clear that Red Holzman was the one coach who most influenced what would become my own vision of the pro game,"[3] said Jackson. One thing he adopted was closing team practices to the media, so that players could learn from their mistakes without the pressure of being reported upon. Another was Red's habit of asking the team during time-outs which offensive plays they should run next, even during critical games. He also let players draw up their own plays. Holzman wouldn't always take players' advice, but he empowered them to become students of the game.

And finally, Holzman gave his reserves a good idea when they would come off the bench and how long they'd be on the court. Phil would adopt this approach, believing it was a waste of energy for a player to maintain focus and intensity without knowing when he'd actually enter the game.

> *"He played every game like it was the seventh game of the playoffs."*[4]
>
> —Danny Randolph

In 1971, when this photo was taken, Jackson's playing time was still limited as he recovered from a career-threatening back injury.

In January 1968, Jackson suffered a serious back injury that required spinal fusion surgery. Anything from a slip of the scalpel to a rash move in rehab would mean the end of his career. He wore a body brace for six months. He missed the rest of that season, and was put on injured reserve the following year to protect him from being selected by new teams in an expansion draft.

Jackson now felt emotionally disconnected from his teammates. But taking a spectator's perspective changed his view of the game. The Knicks were a good team to watch, as Red's squad won the 1970 NBA championship. Watching over Red's shoulder gave Jackson a deeper understanding of the league. Red asked him to break down game tape, identifying opponents' strengths and weaknesses and drawing up their key plays. "Now I began to see basketball as a dynamic game of chess in which all the pieces were in motion," said Jackson. "It was exhilarating."[5]

During this time, Jackson also bought a used BMW motorcycle and road-tripped with his older brother Joe, a psychology professor. Jackson understood the risks of riding, but for him they only made the experience more meaningful. "On a bike, you have to be continuously alert. You can never fall into the kind of trance that you often

Seeing Red

After winning both NBL and NBA championships with the Rochester Royals, Hall-of-Famer Red Holzman was initially a player-coach. He then won 613 games in fifteen years with the Knicks, including two NBA championships. Though he could be an exacting taskmaster, especially on defense, Holzman calmed his players by keeping winning and losing in perspective. A reporter once asked him what he would consider a real disaster. "Coming home and finding we have run out of scotch," [6] Holzman replied.

do when driving a car … You have to be totally present in the environment. It's a very Zen attitude."[7]

On the trip, Jackson visited Montana's Flathead Lake, where as a boy he'd fished with bamboo poles. Feeling powerfully drawn to the place and its Native American history, he vowed to build a home there someday. The experience left Jackson with greater clarity about what he wanted in life and the home on the lake would become an important refuge for him.

FORMING AN IDENTITY

Though Jackson's rehab was long and hard, with many moments of despair, he eventually regained his form on the court. In 1971–72, he averaged sixteen minutes and seven points per game. Nothing special, but it was progress. He also picked up the nicknames "Coat Hanger," "Head and Shoulders" (both due to his build), and, his personal favorite, "Action Jackson," which play-by-play announcer Marv

Albert used during broadcasts. Meanwhile, Jackson's first marriage ended and he became a man about town based in a Chelsea loft, where he entertained often. "I lived the life of a sixties Renaissance man, complete with long hair and jeans," he wrote in his 2013 book *Eleven Rings.* "I loved the freedom and idealism, not to mention the great music, of the countercultural wave that was sweeping through New York and the rest of the country. I bought a bicycle and pedaled all over town, trying to connect with the *real* New York City." [8]

Meanwhile, the Knicks made it back to the NBA Finals, where the Los Angeles Lakers beat them in five games. Around this time Jackson met his second wife, with whom he'd share thirty years. June Perry was an independent spirit and politically radical, more so than Jackson, but a great companion for someone who loved nature and long hikes as much as he did.

With the Knicks of the early '70s, coach Red Holtzman orchestrated an offense famous for its fluidity.

By the 1972–73 season, Jackson was not only a key contributor on the court, he was entrusted with teaching new players both the offense and the Holzman way of doing things: the idea that the team comes first. Their scoring was perfectly balanced, with six players scoring in double figures. "On a good team there are no superstars," said Red. "There are great players who show they are great players by being able to play with others as a team. They have the ability to be superstars, but if they fit into a good team, they make sacrifices, they do things necessary to help the team win."[9] Jackson would later share this thought with Michael Jordan.

During these years, Jackson played with future Hall-of-Famers Willis Reed, Walt "Clyde" Frazier, Earl "the Pearl" Monroe, and Dave DeBusschere. Bill Bradley, who later had a distinguished political career as a US senator, particularly fascinated Jackson. As a rookie, Bradley was always the center of attention but never let it overwhelm him. Jackson wrote that Bradley "was gifted at building consensus among the players and helping them meld together into a team."[10]

In Game Four of the 1973 Eastern Conference Finals, Jackson showed his Zen calm when faced with two critical free throws. The Boston Celtics led by two with eleven seconds left in overtime. Without hesitation, Jackson shot both foul shots the moment the referee handed him the ball. *Swish. Swish.* It was clear that he didn't want to think about what was at stake; he simply wanted to act on instinct. In the second overtime, Jackson made several key plays, and New York notched a decisive win to go up 3–1 in the series.

From there, they finished off Boston and beat the Lakers in five games to win their second ring in five years. This one Jackson earned. As a trusted sixth man, he was the kind of valuable role player he would later identify and acquire to support the stars on his championship teams.

Immediately after the season ended, Jackson jumped on his motorcycle and took a leisurely cross-country road trip. Jackson and two

This 1973 photo from Jackson's heyday with the Knicks shows one incarnation of his ever-changing facial hair. He was a valued member of Red's rotation at the time.

Knicks teammates started a six-year series of basketball clinics on the Pine Ridge Reservation in South Dakota, home to the hoops-loving Lakota Sioux. He was taken with the tribe's philosophy that a person is not merely an individual, but an integral part of the universe. From this point on, Jackson introduced people in his life to the power of Native American culture. For years he returned to the reservation every summer.

Despite his efforts to master his emotions and connect with others through a heightened spiritual awareness, Jackson's competitive drive only grew more intense. Like his future pupil Michael Jordan, he wanted to win at everything, whether it was backgammon, stickball, or his long-running

"If you meet the Buddha in the lane, feed him the ball."[11]

—Phil Jackson

pickup game with friends and former teammates. "He played every game like it was the seventh game of the playoffs,"[12] said Danny Randolph, a member of the group.

In 1973–74, Jackson was playing the best ball of his career and the team made it to the Eastern Conference Finals. He knew enough about every city the Knicks visited to play tour guide. "He was curious about everything," said teammate and longtime friend Neal Walk. "He just had to keep learning." [13]

The following year, the Knicks were ousted in the first round. Their heyday was drawing to a close, Holzman retired in 1977, and gradually the talent waned as time and expansion drafts pulled the team apart. "The roster became so overloaded with scorers and not good passers that our offense got flat," [14] said Jackson.

Jackson's minutes dwindled, and so did the team's wins. He did meet Jim Cleamons, a new teammate who at that time seemed a more natural teacher and coach than Jackson did. "Phil was completely unselfish as a player—I saw that right away," [15] said Cleamons. He would later become an essential part of Jackson's coaching staff.

In Jackson's eleventh season, at age thirty-three, he was clearly on the downslope of his playing career. Traded to the New Jersey Nets in 1978, he considered retirement to rest his aching body and only continued playing because he could stay in New York. This development would prove momentous, because it was his first step on the path to becoming a basketball coach.

The Lakota Way

Phil Jackson embraced the selfless warrior philosophy of the Lakota Sioux. As a coach, he would often share their Great Spirit Prayer with his players. One translation ends this way: *I seek strength not to be superior to my brothers, but to fight my greatest enemy—myself. Make me ever ready to come to you with clean hands and straight eyes. So that when life fades as a fading sunset, my spirit may come to you without shame.*

3

A VAGABOND COACH

- - - - - - - - - - - - - - -

New Jersey Nets coach Kevin Loughery promised Jackson that joining his team would be a bridge from playing to coaching. "I knew he'd be an outstanding coach from the start," said Loughery, citing Jackson's "extreme desire to compete" and adding, "he was ready then. He could have stepped into coaching anywhere."[1] At the time though, Jackson had no desire to complete that transition. His alternatives included law school, a graduate degree in psychology, and the ministry.

Seeing a different team run under a different leader was valuable for Jackson. Loughery ran an ingenious offense. "[This] actually marked the beginning of my long search for the perfect offensive system," said Jackson. "One that would allow a team to play hard and smart. One that would allow freedom while still adhering to a structure."[2]

Often a vocal critic of referees, Loughery was ejected from fourteen games that year, and Jackson usually took over, gaining valuable game experience as a coach. Once, when Loughery threatened to quit, he told the general manager that Jackson should replace him. "For the first time, I was faced with the realization that someone I respected believed I was capable of being a head coach in the NBA,"[3] said Jackson.

Though he didn't feel ready for that job, Jackson returned in 1979–80 to play his last sixteen

San Antonio's George Gervin shoots over Jackson. Though Phil's body was breaking down, he was mentally ready to coach at the pro level.

games in the NBA and work primarily as an assistant coach. After the season, he believed that basketball was now behind him. The feeling that playing the game had given him was irreplaceable. "I was never going to feel the thrill of battle again … Being a coach was not the same, or at least that was how I felt at the time."[4]

He was content to finish the house he'd begun building on Flathead Lake in Montana. He wanted to lead a simple life, one centered around his family. There were flirtations with various jobs, but by this time he had four kids with June. The family business was a small, struggling health club in Kalispell, Montana. Then Jackson got a call from the Albany Patroons, a Continental Basketball Association (CBA) team on the verge of firing its coach with six weeks left in the season. Ironically, the departing coach was one of Jackson's old team-mates on the Knicks, and a Red Holzman-inspired offense was already in place.

The CBA was a respected minor league populated by players almost good enough for the NBA, but not quite. Though Albany was out of the playoff chase, they would host the CBA All-Star game that year, in a quirk of the league's rules. Jackson's Patroons beat the best players from all the other teams, a rare accomplishment. Returning the next season, he put his stamp on the team. Their offense was fluid and their defense relentless. Jackson began or ended practices with medi-tation and prayer circles. He gave players hand-picked books to read, texts he'd found inspiring himself.

> "There's no need to overpower when you can outsmart."[5]
> —Phil Jackson

On road trips, Jackson took the team to historic sites and tribal reservations, to open their minds to the world outside basketball. Driving the team van, a twelve-passenger Dodge Ram, Jackson was like a human GPS. He could remember a complex series of direc-tions, navigating back roads in a completely unfamiliar place, to find a restaurant he'd only heard about. He was also in the habit of doing the *New York Times* crossword puzzle while driving with the dome light on, anchoring the newspaper against the steering wheel. This alarmed players at first, but he proved to be an excellent driver in any weather conditions.

Albany finished second in the conference and then embarked on a stirring playoff run. At halftime of the decisive fifth game of a tied-up CBA championship series, the Patroons were down by fourteen. The players credited Jackson's stirring speech, and a key halftime adjustment, with a comeback win. It was clear that the young coach had what it took. "He had an understanding of the big picture, the flow of the game," said player Derrick Rowland. "But I guess your biggest thing was, you wanted to do it for him … He was the kind of guy you didn't want to let down."[6]

To augment his small CBA paycheck, Jackson took a job coaching in Puerto Rico's summer league. Many NBA coaches cut their teeth there. Basketball was very popular on the island, and at least four games were televised weekly. The rivalries between neighboring towns were ferocious, and home teams rarely lost—officials didn't want to risk angering the local fans, who could be overzealous. For the same reason, the league's

Minor League Made a Major Impact for Some

Founded in 1946, the Continental Basketball Association actually predated the NBA by two months. The CBA functioned as a "feeder league" for the NBA, sometimes producing success stories such as Mario Elie. The gritty swingman went from the Albany Patroons to the Houston Rockets, where he was a key player on two NBA championship teams in the 1990s. In 2000, the NBA severed its relationship with the league and created its own developmental league, a death knell for the CBA.

basketball courts were surrounded by wire fences. If a visiting team did win, sometimes the home fans would hurl rocks at their departing cars.

The main value of this experience, beyond helping Jackson's family pay the bills, was that he became a master of non-verbal communication. He didn't speak Spanish, so he had to find other ways to express himself during games when a translator couldn't assist him. From his ear-piercing whistle, which he used to cut through the noise of a raucous crowd, to the influence of an arched eyebrow, Jackson knew how to get his players' attention.

Back in the CBA, Jackson's Patroons made the playoffs twice more, including a return to the conference finals. After four years of coaching year-round in two leagues, Jackson decided that it was now NBA or nothing. "My future was decidedly unsettled," he said. "I took an aptitude test that accurately reflected my interests in cooking and in outdoor activities, and suggested a career in either the ministry or law."[7] He had faith that the right path would present itself. But Phil sensed that NBA teams held his book, *Maverick*, against him. Not only was he critical of coaches, peers, and the league as a whole, he'd written candidly about players' drug use—including his own.

KRAUSE HAD KEPT AN EYE ON HIM

Jackson still had one champion in the league, and it was Chicago Bulls GM Jerry Krause, who had coveted Jackson as an NBA prospect years prior. In 1987, Krause set up an interview for Jackson with Bulls coach Doug Collins. Knowing this was his last, best opportunity,

In July 1989, Jerry Krause (*right*) announced Jackson as head coach of the Chicago Bulls. Their relationship started out strong but deteriorated over the years.

Jackson nailed it. "He can talk with politicians," said Neal Walk. "He can talk with poverty-stricken people. He can ride limos, motorcycles, bicycles."[8]

In Chicago, his fellow assistant coaches Tex Winter (offense) and Johnny Bach (defense) would become new mentors for Jackson. The Bulls were also rich in talent on the court. They had the incomparable Michael Jordan, who'd dropped sixty-three points on the Boston Celtics in a losing effort the previous spring (his season average was a whopping thirty-seven). They also had a remarkably versatile pair of forwards in Scottie Pippen, who could literally do it all, and Horace Grant, a great rebounder who could also score. All three were capable of playing smothering defense.

Jackson was charged with scouting opponents and coaching big man Brad Sellers, in whom Collins had little confidence. "Phil looked for the positive," said Sellers. "He'd just say, 'this is what I need you to do,' clear and concise, in a way that makes you say, 'okay, I can do that for you.' And you did. Even if you had to look up some of his words to see what they meant."[9]

That season the Bulls won ten more games than the year before, but they were mauled in the playoffs by the Detroit Pistons, a deep and extremely physical team dubbed "the Bad Boys" for their tendency to willingly pick up fouls with a punishing defense. It was a disappointing end to the year for a talented team.

In December 1988, the Bulls were just one game over a .500 record. With the Bulls down by double figures to an equally average Milwaukee Bucks team, the officials ejected Doug Collins. Jackson took over, as he had in New Jersey years earlier. At halftime, Jackson called for a full-court press and a more improvisational offense. From there, Chicago outscored Milwaukee 66–38 and won easily. After Detroit beat them again in the playoffs, Collins was fired. Two months before his forty-fourth birthday, Phil Jackson took over the top job.

Jackson's calm, controlled demeanor was a far cry from

Originators of an Artful Offense

Morice "Tex" Winter had a sixty-one-year coaching career. After serving in the Navy during World War II, he attended USC and learned the Triangle offense from its originator, legendary multi-sport coach Sam Barry. Becoming a coach himself, Winter had great success with the Triangle on the college level and published a seminal text on the subject (*The Triple-Post Offense*, 1962). As Jackson's former player Mark Madsen put it, "The Triangle is a decision tree … Literally a thousand different things could happen on any one trip down the court."[10] In 2011, Winter was voted into the Naismith Basketball Hall of Fame.

Tex Winter (*left*) became Jackson's most trusted advisor on coaching staffs in Chicago and Los Angeles. Winter's candid, "tell it like it is" approach often offered a dissenting voice that Jackson valued.

Collins, a fiery, high-energy coach. Collins used a thick, ever-growing playbook and generally dictated everything the team did. By contrast, Jackson would rely heavily on Winter and Bach as assistant coaches, while giving players final say on the court through the Triangle offense. Another addition to the staff was offensive mind Jim Cleamons, who would scout opponents and provide players with individual instruction.

> *"His aura precedes him."*[11]
> —Craig Hodges

Jackson's practices stressed defense. He was fortunate that his two best offensive players, Jordan and Pippen, were also otherworldly talents on the other side of the floor. They guarded each other in practice, which only made them better. The pair did not read the books Jackson gave them, but three-point specialist Craig Hodges called his assignment, Dan Millman's *Way of the Peaceful Warrior,* an "eye opener." Hodges took to the Triangle immediately, which he likened to the style of play instinctively utilized in pickup games. That season Hodges hit eighty-seven three's and won the long-range competition at the All-Star Game. He also took to Jackson. "His aura precedes him," said Hodges. "He's not *trying* to be charismatic, or knowledgeable, or a leader. He just is." [12]

Jackson's first Bulls team opened the regular season 21–9 and closed on a 17–3 run. While Chicago won its first two postseason series, the playoffs presented the inevitable obstacle of the Pistons in the Eastern Conference Finals. Playing with a migraine in the decisive Game Seven, Pippen shot one for ten, and Detroit cruised to a 93–74 win. "It was my most difficult moment as a coach," [13] said Jackson, years later.

That team drew twenty thousand more fans than the year before, won five more games, and made it to the brink of the NBA Finals. It had been a great year for Chicago, but beating the Detroit Pistons was more than a goal for the 1990–91 season—it was an imperative, for players and coaches alike.

4

COULD THE "BAD BOYS" BE BEATEN?

T o Jackson's eye, Michael Jordan showed up at training camp look-ing bigger and stronger. Jackson still hadn't gotten Jordan's full acceptance of the Triangle, which the superstar derisively referred to as the "equal-opportunity offense." Jordan was reticent to embrace a quirky democratic system designed to spread the ball around because his teammates had yet to convince him they could take advantage of their opportunities. The only players he trusted to score were Scottie Pippen, his sidekick, and John Paxson, one of the most reliable jump shooters. "I understand that," Jackson told Jordan. "But I think if you give the system a chance, they'll learn to be playmakers … You can't beat a good defensive team with one man. It's got to be a team effort."[1]

"If I was going to have any success realizing my vision for the team, I knew my first challenge was to win over Michael Jordan,"[2] said Jackson. He told Jordan the last player to win the scoring title and a championship in the same year was Kareem Abdul-Jabbar, in 1971.

Meanwhile Jackson tinkered with the Triangle in hopes of perfecting the Bulls' attack. "What I was looking for was the middle path between Tex [Winter's] purity and Michael [Jordan's] creativity,"[4] said Jackson. It worked, and it didn't diminish Jordan's scoring: in 1990–91 he averaged 31.5 points, best in the NBA, and was named league MVP for the second time. "Every now and then Michael would break loose and take over a game," said Jackson. "But that didn't bother me as long as it didn't become a habit. I knew he needed bursts of creativity to keep from getting bored, and that his solo performances would strike terror in the hearts of our enemies, not to mention help win some key games."[5]

> "[Jordan] was Michelangelo in baggy shorts."[3]
>
> —Phil Jackson

Jackson also created a new position for Pippen: "point forward." Before a huge growth spurt, Pippen played the point in high school and could deftly handle the ball with either hand. Pippen later said this shift "made me the player I wanted to be in the NBA."[6] The move made Chicago's fast break positively lethal, with Jordan leading the attack on transition and Pippen flying down the floor a few steps behind. Pippen was also a willing passer, which created opportunities for what Jordan called his "supporting cast."

COULD THE "BAD BOYS" BE BEATEN?

Jackson introduced his team to traditional Lakota customs to provide focus and community. Before practice he had players gather in a circle to discuss the day's objectives. When he wanted them to convene for a meeting, he beat a drum. After a bad loss, he'd burn sage to purify the locker room. Jackson didn't take himself or these rituals too seriously, but he saw real value in them. The team was becoming a cohesive unit before his eyes. That transformation's value to a basketball coach was, as Jackson biographer Peter Richmond put it, that "The Sioux respect the tribe before the individual."[8]

The meeting room was a sacred space decorated with Native American totems and other symbolic objects Jackson had collected. "I had the room decorated this way to reinforce in the players' minds that our journey together each year, from the start of training camp to the last whistle of the playoffs, is a sacred quest," said Jackson. "This is the room where the spirit of the team takes form."[9]

Jackson also taught the players an abbreviated version of the Zen meditations he'd been practicing for years. Even if some of them

A Tough Place to Play

Opened in 1929, Chicago Stadium earned the monikers "Madhouse on Madison," for the frenzies of its home fans, and "The Big Barn," for its shape. Its steep, close-to-the-action balconies and small size—four Chicago Stadiums could fit inside its replacement, the 960,000 square-foot United Center—made it one of the loudest arenas in the NBA. The noise fans made was deafening, with measurements reaching 130 decibels (140 is an aircraft carrier's deck). Michael Jordan calculated the home-court advantage as "ten points, at least."[7]

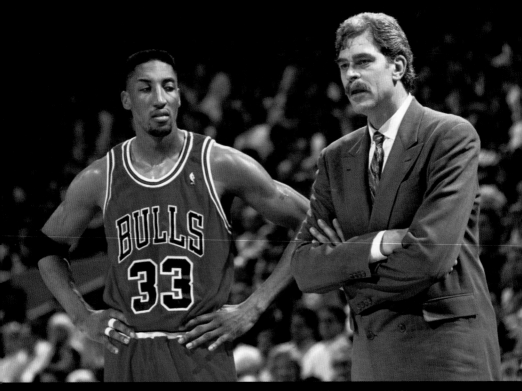

It can be argued that the versatility of Scottie Pippen (#33) was as vital to the Bulls' glory years as Michael Jordan's scoring. Pippen presented a mismatch offensively and defensively.

napped, Jackson liked getting the players to relax for ten minutes before watching game tape. "The experience of sitting quietly together in a group tends to bring about a subtle shift in consciousness that strengthens the team bond,"[10] said Jackson.

Jackson's larger goal was to get them to take a more mindful approach to the game, being as present as possible without becoming distracted by thoughts of the past or future. "The point is to perform every activity, from playing basketball to taking out the garbage, with precise attention, moment by moment," Jackson explained in his book *Sacred Hoops.* "For some people, notably Michael Jordan, the only impetus they need to become completely focused is intense competition. But for most of us, athletes and non-athletes alike, the battle itself is not enough. Many players I've worked with tend to *lose* their equanimity after a certain point as the level of competition rises, because their minds start racing out of control."[11] Jackson says he was that kind of player himself, which led him to his meditation practice.

THESE BULLS COULDN'T BE BEATEN AT "THE BIG BARN"

Early in the season, Chicago's swarming defense held the Cleveland Cavaliers to five points in a quarter. Just before the All-Star Break, they won eighteen out of nineteen games, including a visit to the Pistons' "Palace of Auburn Hills." The Bulls hadn't won there since Game 1 of the 1989 playoffs.

With the significant home-court advantage Chicago Stadium provided, the Bulls reeled off twenty-six straight wins at "The Big Barn" en route to a 61–21 overall record. Chicago swept New York in the first round of the playoffs and lost only one game to the Philadelphia 76ers before seeking redemption against the team that had ousted them from the playoffs three years in a row. The Pistons entered the series with key injuries, but even at full strength they would have had their hands full. Though the Bulls were poised and played aggressively, they would not be baited into Detroit's brawling style of ball. "Players were tackled, tripped, elbowed and smacked in the face," said Jackson. "But they all laughed it off. The Pistons didn't know how to respond. We completely disarmed them by not striking back. At that moment, our players became true champions." [12] The Bulls swept the Bad Boys and went on to play the Los Angeles Lakers in the NBA Finals.

From a TV ratings perspective, it was a matchup made in heaven: "Michael versus Magic." Jordan was keenly aware that he was in his seventh year without a championship, while Magic Johnson had won five in his first nine seasons.

Wondrous Hardwood Wizardry

Drafted first overall in 1979, Magic Johnson took the NBA by storm. He immediately became a leader on a Lakers team loaded with veterans, and he was so instrumental in L.A. winning the 1980 title that he was the first rookie to win the Finals MVP award. Magic's Lakers won four more championships in the '80s. Before the 1991–1992 season he suddenly retired, announcing that he had HIV. Nonetheless, Magic played in the 1992 NBA All-Star game, was a member of the gold-medal-winning US Olympic team that year, and averaged almost fifteen points in the thirty-six games he played for the Lakers in a 1995–1996 comeback.

In Game 1, the best defense belonged to the Lakers, while Magic had a triple double (19–11–10). Still, it took Sam Perkins' three-pointer with fourteen seconds left to give Los Angeles the winning margin. Jackson noticed that whenever Magic came out of the game, the Bulls' second unit gained ground. To tire out Magic, Jackson put Pippen on him in Game 2 and the course of the series changed. At six-foot-seven (201 cm), the forward had the length to cover Magic, even though Magic was actually two inches taller. Magic missed nine of his thirteen shots. Meanwhile,

Pippen dished out ten assists and scored twenty points as the Bulls won with authority, 107–86.

The series shifted from Chicago to Los Angeles, but the momentum stayed with the Bulls. In Game 3, Jordan forced overtime with 3.4 seconds left, and his team pulled away to win 104–96 and silence fans at the "Fabulous" Forum in

Jordan and the Bulls came up short in this 1989 game against Detroit, but by the next season they were ready to beat "the Bad Boys" and compete for a championship.

Inglewood. Game 4 was a great defensive effort for the Bulls, who held L.A. to their lowest point total since 1954. Jordan publicly credited Bill Cartwright, to whom he'd been slow to warm up. The creaky old center with the eternally pensive expression, salt-and-pepper goatee, and sharp elbows was a stalwart presence in the lane. "He was like a big brother," said Paxson. "If someone was picking on you, he was going to make sure you knew he was there looking out for you."[13]

In Game 5, Jordan went back to his trigger-happy ways, despite the fact that Paxson was consistently open.

> *"The feeling of connection when players pull together is a tremendous force that can wipe away the fear of losing."*[14]
>
> —Phil Jackson

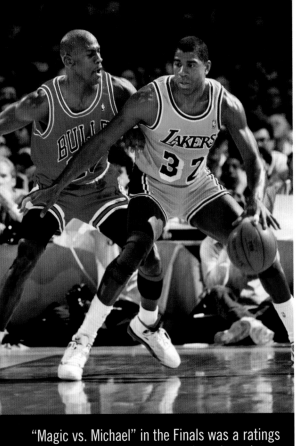

"Magic vs. Michael" in the Finals was a ratings bonanza as it pitted a five-time champion against the NBA's latest and greatest phenom.

During a timeout, Jackson asked the huddle, "Who's open?" and Jordan saw his point. In crunch time, His Airness would drive and draw the defense to him, then kick the ball out to an open Paxson. The sharpshooter hit a flurry of jumpers in the fourth quarter to seal the deal in a 108–101, series-clinching victory.

In a far cry from the end of the previous year, Pippen's season ended with thirty-two points in a win, and Jordan had finally bought into "Phil-osophy." As MJ put it, "In the fourth quarter, your leadership, your unity, your understanding of personnel, your fulfillment of roles—all those things come out. And I think that's the way we won."[15]

While teams love to win a championship in front of their home crowd, for Jackson there was a resonance to winning his first (NBA) ring as a coach on the road. Jackson's Knicks had celebrated in the same visitors' locker room back in 1973, when he helped New York defeat Los Angeles in the Finals. A circle had been completed.

5

BIRTH OF A DYNASTY

Jackson said that to win a championship, a team must "embrace a vision in which the group imperative takes precedence over individual glory."[1] The 1991 NBA champions had learned that lesson. Within weeks, however, the road to repeat had grown rocky. Jackson was concerned. "[Legendary UCLA coach] John Wooden used to say that 'winning takes talent, to repeat takes character.' I didn't really understand what he meant until we started our second run for the ring … As Jordan put it, 'Success turns we's back into me's.'"[2]

To make matters worse, *Chicago Tribune* reporter Sam Smith had recently published *The Jordan Rules*, a tell-all book that aired the team's dirty laundry. The book portrayed Michael as an egomaniac who delighted in mocking everyone around him. "Michael was furious when it appeared, but in a strange way, it had a liberating effect on

Young Michael Jordan didn't trust his teammates to do what he could do better: score. They would earn that trust, and Jackson's Triangle offense actually made it easier for His Airness to pile up the points.

him," said Phil. "He realized that he didn't have to be Mr. Perfect all the time, and that freed him to find out who he really was."[3] Jordan's jibes were intended to coax forth his teammates' best efforts. "I don't take things too seriously," said Jordan. "I'm able to laugh at myself before I laugh at anybody else … But then I can be hard [on others]."[4]

Smith's book also contained a number of unflattering anecdotes about one of Jordan's favorite targets for ridicule, Jerry Krause, which caused the excitable, eccentric executive to fly

> *"If you give the future all your attention, the present will pass you by."*[5]
>
> —**Phil Jackson**

into a rage. He went on a witch hunt to find out who within the team had told these "lies." As one of Smith's sources, Jackson said, "The way I handled Jerry was to keep things light. I knew that his overreaction to *The Jordan Rules* stemmed from his feeling that he wasn't getting the credit he deserved for building this great team. I understood. But I couldn't fix it, so I tried to shift his mind with a touch of humor and compassion."[6]

When training camp began, Jackson got the team refocused on basketball. "I redoubled my efforts to turn practice into a sanctuary from the messiness of the outside world," he said. "As the team turned its attention inward, the bond among the players began to re-form."[7]

Chicago opened the year 37–5 before losing four of five games in January. By March the Bulls were back in fine form, winning nineteen of their last twenty-one games to complete the 1991–1992 schedule at 67–15, the best record in franchise history. MJ won his sixth-straight scoring crown and third league MVP award. Pippen was All-NBA second-team.

"Pip" Elevated Every Team He Was a Part Of

The youngest of twelve children, Scottie Pippen was a shy kid born in Hamburg, Arkansas, a town with a population under 3,000. He didn't start on his high school team until his senior year and was not initially offered a scholarship at the University of Central Arkansas—he paid tuition with a grant to be the team's equipment manager and made the team as a "walk-on." For two summers he did welding work in furniture plants before a growth spurt turned him into a basketball beast. In the NBA, Pippen made the playoffs sixteen straight times. He was inducted into the Hall of Fame in 2010.

A MUCH STEEPER CLIMB THIS TIME

Jackson thought they could easily have won seventy games that year, but he wanted the team to enter the playoffs as healthy and rested as possible, so he made liberal use of his bench. As it turned out, they needed every iota of energy they had conserved to make it through this playoff minefield. The Bulls swept the Miami Heat in the first round, but the new-look Knicks posed a much greater problem. Now coached by Pat Riley, with whom Jackson had often sparred in the media, New York had taken over the Pistons' mantle as the league's most physically punishing team to play against.

In the crucial Game 5, Air Jordan took to the sky, attacking the rim over and over again. On many drives he was fouled, and he converted all fifteen of his free throws to make New York pay. He finished with thirty-seven points, and Chicago won, 96–88. At Madison Square Garden New York's John Starks, a quick, hard-driving guard, came off the bench to score twenty-seven points and force a Game 7 back in Chicago. Michael scored forty-two, Scottie notched a triple-double, and the Bulls' defense rose to another level. Chicago prevailed, 110–81.

The Cleveland Cavaliers were no pushovers, either. The Eastern Conference Finals opened 2–2 before Chicago could take control and close out the Cavs. "Last year was the honeymoon," Jackson told reporters after the series. "This year was an odyssey."[8]

The Portland Trail Blazers had reached the cusp of the Finals the previous season, but the Lakers managed to defeat them. Now they'd taken the next step and were ready to seize the league's throne.

Shooting guard Clyde "the Glide" Drexler drew comparisons to Jordan, which Michael didn't appreciate. In Game 1, Jordan came out on fire from the field, and he just kept taking three-pointers until he'd made six of them. "I was in a zone," Jordan said. "My threes felt like free throws. I didn't know what I was doing, but they were going in."[9] His almost apologetic shrug, palms up, became the signature image of a 122–89 win for Chicago.

MJ was "in the zone" against Portland in Game 1 of the Finals, hitting six of ten from long range. His three-point prowess that night amazed even him.

Game 2 went the other way as Portland staged a fourth-quarter comeback to force overtime. Jordan missed a potential game-winner at the buzzer, a rare occurrence for the preternaturally clutch player. Nine points from marksman Danny Ainge in overtime produced a 115–104 Portland win. Happy to have a split after two games in Chicago, the Trail Blazers looked forward to three home games.

"More than anything, I wanted to build a team that would blend individual talent with a heightened group consciousness."[10]

—Phil Jackson

Jackson believed the outcome of Game 3 hinged on the travel plans of both teams. The Blazers returned home immediately after Game 2, while the Bulls slept in their own beds before making the long cross-country flight. (Jackson felt his foe in the 1996 Finals, George Karl, made the same tactical error after Game 2 in Chicago.) Portland came out flat at home, and Chicago took Game 3.

Stern Knew How to Brighten Stars

When David Stern became NBA commissioner in 1984, the league was foundering. The Finals drew half the TV ratings the World Series did, and the NFL was pulling ahead, too. While talents such as Michael Jordan, Hakeem Olajuwon, and Charles Barkley did arrive the same year, Stern became a master marketer for the NBA brand and its history. He left the league in a vastly better place than he found it. As journalist David Aldridge put it, "David Stern ruled the NBA for 30 years with a velvet glove, iron fist, breathtaking intellect, inexhaustible work ethic, a personal sense of right and wrong, and a love for basketball." [11]

A see-saw series continued with Portland winning the next one, but Jordan went off again in Game 5. As he had against New York, MJ attacked the basket relentlessly and hit sixteen of his nineteen free throws. He finished with forty-six points, and Chicago left Portland with a 119–106 win.

Facing elimination at the Madhouse on Madison, the Blazers played inspired ball, and the Bulls found themselves in a seventeen-point hole late in the third quarter. Jackson rolled out his reserves alongside Pippen, and they played with great energy and enthusiasm. Plucky benchwarmer Scott Hansen hit a big three, stole a pass, and fed Pippen for another bucket to force a Portland timeout. The rally was on as Jordan cheered from the bench. After Hansen, B. J. Armstrong, and Scott Williams sparked a 14–2 Bulls run, Jordan returned and scored twelve of his thirty-three points. The home crowd got to celebrate both a series-clinching 97–93 win and the Bulls' back-to-back NBA championships. "For me, this was the sweetest victory because *everybody* on the team made a significa-tion contribution,"[12] said Jackson.

That summer, Jordan and Pippen went to Barcelona, Spain, to play for the 1992 US Olympic Team. Dubbed the "Dream Team," the star-studded roster featured Magic Johnson, Larry Bird, Charles Barkley, and David Robinson, among others. In Barcelona, Pippen took his game up a notch, proving that his versatility was unique even on a team of elite players. Jordan came back raving about Pippen's play and conceded that his sidekick had outshone him at times.

6

AN EARLY END TO AN ERA

- - - - - - - - - - - -

Entering the 1992–1993 season the Bulls had two captains: Jordan, for obvious reasons, and Cartwright, for the veteran's stabilizing presence in the locker room. But Pippen lacked the title in name only. While Michael led by example and motivational barbs, Pippen provided teammates with a patient, nurturing presence they needed. The pecking order was clear and unquestioned. "Phil was the centerpiece of the team, and I was an extension of that centerpiece," said Jordan. "He relied on me to connect with all the different personalities on the team … He and I had a great bond, so everything I did, Scottie did, and then it fell down the line … Nothing could get inside that circle."[1]

Another important player joined the Bulls that year. Shooting guard Steve Kerr was no one's idea of a star, but he had the same knack for clutch shooting that Paxson did. He had the mental toughness to play on a Michael Jordan team, where weakness wasn't tolerated, and he earned MJ's respect after an on-court tussle. Kerr was struck by the unique culture Jackson had created, a culture from which he'd borrow aspects in his own coaching career years later. As Paxson described it, "It felt as if we were part of something really important. We felt like the good guys because we were trying to play the game the right way."[2]

The 1992–93 edition of the Bulls was not as dominant as the last, however. Cartwright (thirty-five) and Paxson (thirty-two) had had offseason knee surgeries and weren't themselves. Pippen battled an ankle injury most of the season. Even Jordan had foot issues and felt dogged by the invasive media; he seemed tired of it all.

The banged-up Bulls won "just" fifty-seven games and did not earn home-court advantage throughout the playoffs. Jordan did lead the league in scoring for the seventh straight time, tying Wilt Chamberlain's record. But Jackson had to

Pat's Teams Could Be Polished or Pugnacious

Though Pat Riley hailed from hardscrabble Schenectady, New York, he became famous for sleek Armani suits during his time as the Lakers' young coach in their "Showtime" era. After four championships, Pat stepped down as the most famous coach in the league. Guiding the Knicks down a different path, Riley built a bruising, methodical team that reached the Finals and netted him a second Coach of the Year award. Moving on to the Miami Heat, Riley coached a championship team he built around Shaquille O'Neal and Dwyane Wade. As team president, he acquired LeBron James and Chris Bosh to join Wade in "the Big Three," winning two more titles.

push more psychological buttons to get the team focused and in rhythm for the playoffs.

The switch flipped, however. Chicago swept Atlanta and Cleveland. The Bulls then flew to New York for Game 1 with the Knicks. The home team's brutish brand of defense held Jordan to ten of twenty-seven shooting in a 98–90 New York win. He then missed twenty of thirty-two shots in Game 2. John Starks punctuated his passionate performance with a dunk over Jordan with forty-seven seconds left, capping the Knicks' five-point win. The Bulls found themselves down 2–0 and dirt was thrown on their graves, at least in the New York media.

Making matters worse was a *New York Times* column about Jordan gambling in Atlantic City in the wee hours before Game 2. Suddenly reporters latched onto the notion that Jordan had a gambling addiction, and the entire team stopped talking to the media. "We don't need a curfew," Jackson told reporters, "These are adults. You have to have other things in your life or the pressure becomes too great."[4]

> *"Before a vision can become reality, it must be owned by every single member of the group."*[3]
>
> —Phil Jackson

Jackson did everything he could to ensure the swirling gossip did not distract his team. In Game 3, the Bulls tightened the screws defensively, Pippen took charge offensively, and Chicago won big, 103–83. Then Jordan scored fifty-four to power his team to a 105–95 win. In Game 5, he had a triple-double (29–10–14). In an unforgettable sequence late in the fourth quarter, New York's Charles Smith went up for a game-winning layup, but Grant blocked it. Smith got the ball back, Jordan stripped it, Smith recovered and tried again … only to be rejected from behind, this time by Pippen. Now up 3–2, the Bulls hosted New York for Game 6. Scottie hit a corner jumper and a three to knock out the Knicks, 96–88.

After a trying season, winning the 1993 NBA title triggered an outpouring of relief for Jordan (*center*) and the Bulls.

JOY AND PAIN

In the NBA Finals, Chicago faced a Phoenix Suns team led by Charles Barkley, who was at the height of his career and won the league MVP award that season. Phoenix had the league's best record and lightning-quick point guard Kevin "KJ" Johnson, a terror on the fast break and the future mayor of Sacramento. Swingman "Thunder Dan" Majerle had a knack for hitting the timely trifecta.

Chicago's pressure trapped KJ in the backcourt, and they bottled up Barkley. Meanwhile, the Bulls' pair of superstars combined for fifty-eight points. In Game 2, Barkley equaled Jordan's point total, forty-two, but the Bulls' D stymied KJ and Majerle.

The series shifted back to Chicago with Jackson's guys possessing a seemingly insurmountable advantage at home. But the Suns outlasted them in a 129–121 triple-overtime affair in which their offense came alive. Jordan scored at will in Game 4, putting up fifty-five, and B. J. Armstrong made a late steal to secure the 111–105 win. Perhaps overly eager to close out the Suns, Jordan and Pippen dominated the offense with forty-nine shot attempts in Game 5. But the Phoenix defense stiffened, sending the series back to the Valley of the Sun. Undaunted, Jordan chomped a foot-long cigar as they boarded the plane. "Hello, world champs," he said. "Let's go to Phoenix and kick some [butt]."[5]

Sometimes Jackson had to remind the Bulls (especially Jordan) to run the Triangle. Jackson could say a lot with gestures, expressions, or just a stare.

His confidence was contagious. In Game 6, the Bulls combined for nine three pointers and an 87–79 lead entering the final period. Then they went cold. In the fourth quarter, Phoenix surged to a 98–94 lead. With thirty-eight seconds to play, Jordan brought the Bulls' total to 96, single-handedly scoring Chicago's only nine points of the quarter up to the final play. With fourteen seconds to go, Phil called time-out and when play resumed, Jordan drew the defense to him and passed the ball to Pippen, who drove and dished it off to Grant. The power forward could have tried to muscle his way in for a dunk, but he saw Paxson all by himself beyond the three-point line. "Without hesitating, he made a selfless play instead of trying to be a hero,"[6] said Jackson. Grant whipped the ball over to his team-mate, who drilled a decisive trey.

"It was like a dream come true," Paxson said of his game-winner. "You're a kid out in your driveway shooting shots to 'win champion-ships.' I think it allowed people to relate to that experience, because there are a lot of kids and adults who lived out their own fantasies in their backyards."[7]

"It wasn't the shot that captivated me, however," Jackson wrote in *Eleven Rings*. "It was the pass from Michael that led to the pass from

Swing and a Miss

In 1994, Bulls owner Jerry Reinsdorf's MLB team, the Chicago White Sox, signed Michael Jordan to a minor league contract. Jordan played primarily for Double-A affiliate the Birmingham Barons and was a mediocre player even at that level. He hadn't played baseball since his senior year of high school, thirteen years earlier. *Sports Illustrated*'s Steve Wulf wrote, "Michael Jordan has no more business patrolling right field in Comiskey Park than [former White Sox player] Minnie Minoso has bringing the ball upcourt for the Bulls." Jordan countered, "Believe in what you believe in and make an attempt at it; don't give up before you even try."[8]

Scottie that led to the pass from Horace … That night the Triangle was a thing of beauty."[9]

That night, the Bulls joined the Minneapolis Lakers and Boston Celtics as one of the only teams in NBA history to win three consecutive championships. Paxson said this accomplishment proved that the Chicago Bulls were more than MJ and Scottie. "We all became a little more noticed as players," he said. "That's the greatest part about winning, is how you feel as a group. You're happy for one another. You look at small plays in a game, the people who come off the bench and provide something the group needs … It's not just the best player. It's from one to twelve, the coaches included, and your appreciation for each is very high."[11]

> "People have to learn that nothing lasts forever."[10]
> —Michael Jordan

While Michael Jordan made it look easy on the court, behind the scenes he was always working to imbue his team with will, mental strength, and desire. He was a different kind of leader than his coach—Jordan had to outwork and outperform everyone to be as demanding as he was. The grind was getting to him.

Two weeks after the Finals, Jordan's father, James, was shot and killed after two men (later convicted of the crime) found him napping in his car along a South Carolina road. Somehow this random, indiscriminate act fed conspiracy theories about Jordan's gambling and the NBA. Shattered by grief and stalked by celebrity journalists, Jordan released a statement showing the depth of his outrage at the associations. "These totally unsubstantiated reports reflect a complete lack of sensitivity to basic human decency," it declared. Jackson and Jordan met in the fall and Jordan said he had no motivation to slog through another season. The closest Jackson came to trying to talk him out of it was saying it was sad to deprive the world of watching Jordan play. "I walked away with the understanding that Phil was a great friend," said Jordan. "He made me think about a lot of different things, and didn't let me rush into the decision. But he totally understood that … I had gotten to a point where I was battling a lot of demons rather than focusing on basketball."[12]

Jordan made it official on October 6, 1993. At age thirty, he was calling it quits. His teammates stood by the podium during his press conference. "That was true respect," said Jordan. "They didn't have to be there. They didn't have to show tears. You can't make those things up. I think it sealed the relationship between us."[13] Soon thereafter, Jordan announced that he was going to pursue his late father's dream for him and play professional baseball. "Looking back on it, it was a beautiful thing Michael did," said Jackson. "What a risk he took."[14]

7

LIFE WITHOUT MIKE

- - - - - - - - - - - - - - - - -

Entering a Jordan-less season, Jackson knew his team would have to evolve. "The challenge was not to try to repeat ourselves but to use what we had learned to re-create ourselves—to conjure up a new vision for *this* team … Losing Michael presented a major challenge for me, though not an entirely unwelcome one. What's exciting about coaching is the building process, not the ongoing maintenance work required once your team has achieved success."[1] He was eager to find out if his approach to the game would work without Jordan's magnificence in the middle of it.

The Bulls' Vegas odds of winning a fourth championship plunged, and the sports media speculated that thirty wins would be ambitious. Replacing MJ in the starting lineup was journeyman Pete Meyers, a scrappy player but a far cry from the world's greatest. Meyers' scoring average in seven NBA seasons was 3.8 points per game.

Though the rest of the team's core returned, Bill Cartwright and John Paxson were on their last legs. Newcomer Toni Kukoc was a six-foot-eleven (211 cm) forward who could handle the ball like a guard. Too often, Kukoc asserted his individuality at the team's

> *"Mindfulness is remembering to come back to the present moment."*[2]
>
> —Zen teacher Thich Nhat Hanh

expense, so Jackson was hard on him in practice. "He was used to a more freewheeling style of basketball in Europe and was frustrated by the constraints of the Triangle offense,"[3] said Jackson. "Toni's playful meanderings around the court often defied logic."[4]

They also had Steve Kerr, whose proficiency from long range was unparalleled, and a lightly regarded backup center named Bill Wennington. Jackson told Wennington that once Cartwright was fully healthy he would probably be cut, but Wennington continued to prove his worth. He would spend six seasons in Chicago.

Kerr Becomes a Fine Coach

On his way to five rings (two with San Antonio), Steve Kerr hit a higher percentage of his three-pointers than any player in NBA history (250 attempts or more). After his playing career, he was a team executive with the Phoenix Suns before becoming the coach of the Golden State Warriors, where he won two more championships. Kerr has credited Phil Jackson with, among other things, showing him how to manage a deep bench. "Phil was a genius with that, in terms of keeping guys engaged and motivated," said Kerr. "There's a real power in playing a lot of people because everybody just feels more a part of it and more engaged."[5]

Jackson brought in George Mumford, a sports psychologist and meditation teacher. Mumford's goal is to help athletes experience what psychologists refer to as "flow" or "the zone," a state in which they are completely absorbed by what they are doing and experience a feeling of energized focus. Players describe being "in the zone" as functioning at their highest level possible. "The members of the 1993–94 team were especially receptive," said Jackson. "They wanted to prove to the world that they could be more than Michael's supporting cast and win a championship on their own."[6]

After a rocky start—the team opened the year 6–7—they got healthier and more cohesive. To everyone's surprise, Wennington went toe to toe with future Hall-of-Famer Hakeem Olajuwon, scoring nineteen points and earning a larger role on the court. Chicago was 34–13 at the All-Star break, with Horace Grant and B. J. Armstrong playing in their first All-Star Game. It was clear to the league that the three-time defending champions were not going down without a fight.

In fact, Chicago finished with fifty-five wins and made short work of Cleveland in the first round before facing their Eastern Conference nemesis, New York, in the semifinals. "We'd used more energy to get wins than we'd ever had to use in the past," said Jackson. "How much did we have left for the playoffs?"[7]

Chicago blew a fifteen-point lead in Game 1 and Phil felt the team's newcomers were intimidated by the Knicks, the crowd at Madison Square Garden, and the city as a whole. The next day he cancelled practice and took the whole team on a Staten Island Ferry ride, so he could point out the boroughs, tell the story of the Statue of Liberty, and relax the players. "Phil is great," said Wennington. "The team was really stressed and we were feeling down, and it was … like, 'You know what? We know what we have to do. Let's go and forget about it for two hours, have fun, get our minds straight.'"[8]

"I like to do the unpredictable every now and then to keep the players from getting stale,"[9] said Jackson. Alas, the impromptu ferry ride did not produce a win in Game 2. Back on their home floor, the Bulls managed a 102–102 tie with 1.8 seconds left. Jackson told his team that Kukoc would take the potentially game-winning shot. The "Croatian Sensation" had won five games that season on buzzer-beaters. Pippen had missed three of his four shots in the quarter, but he felt betrayed that Jackson didn't call a play for him in that situation. Scottie said he wasn't going back in the game.

Jackson was surprised, and saddened. "He had broken one of the unspoken rules of sports, and I wasn't sure if his teammates, not to mention the media, would ever forgive him," Jackson wrote in *Sacred Hoops*. "I couldn't remember Scottie ever challenging one of my decisions. He was one of the most selfless players on the team. That's why I had named him a co-captain after Michael retired. But none of that mattered now. In a rash moment, he had violated the trust of his teammates."[10]

The play went on without Pippen, Kukoc hit the shot, and the Bulls won. "In the heat of the game, I simply tried to stay in the moment and make decisions based on what was actually happening," Jackson said. "Rather than asserting my ego and inflaming the situation further, I did what needed to be done: find someone to throw in the ball and go for the win. Afterward, rather than trying to fix things myself, I let the players solve the problem."[11]

In the locker room Cartwright, tears streaming down his face, confronted Pippen in front of everyone. "I can't believe you'd do this to us after everything we've been through together," he said, more heartbroken than angry. "This is our chance to do it on our own, without Michael, and you blow it with your selfishness. I've never been so disappointed in my whole life."[12] Cartwright's wife would

Jackson signs copies of his 2013 book *Eleven Rings*. At each stage of his storied career, he took the time to cowrite a book and share his lessons learned up to that point.

later tell June Jackson that, in fifteen years of marriage, she had never seen her husband cry.

Scottie apologized right then and there. "Those are the moments in games that you live for,"[13] Pippen said later, about the last-second shot. With the exception of Jerry Krause, everyone associated with the team knew this momentary lapse of judgment was out of character for Scottie. Yet Krause became determined to trade him. After the game, the media pilloried Pippen, calling for Chicago to suspend him, but Jackson moved on without punishing his star, once he saw that Pippen would let it go and move on.

The Bulls won by twelve in Game 4 to tie the series. Pippen led the way with twenty-five points, eight rebounds, and six assists. All was forgiven. "I wish there was a fairy-tale ending to this story, but the plot took another bizarre turn,"[14] Jackson wrote in *Eleven Rings.* In Game 5, Chicago was up by one in the final seconds when a questionable foul call from referee Hue Hollins put New York's Hubert Davis on the line for two free throws. He hit both and the Knicks notched a series-tilting win, going up 3–2.

"We [then] beat the Knicks decisively in Game 6, but the fairy tale ended in Game 7," said Jackson.[15] In *Sacred Hoops* he wrote, "That was my favorite season that we didn't come away with a trophy. I was pleased with the way the players transcended the loss of Jordan and turned themselves into a real team ... [The veterans] expected to win the big ones, even when outgunned, and that alone often carried them to victory."[16]

"I'M BACK"

That offseason, Paxson retired, Cartwright signed with Seattle, and Grant joined the Orlando Magic. The Bulls moved into their vast new home, the United Center, and never shot as well there as they had at Chicago Stadium. Krause pressured Jackson to fire Johnny Bach, believing he was the leak responsible for the "slander" in *The Jordan Rules*. By then, Jackson thought Bach would be better off elsewhere, but his trusted assistant's departure dispirited Jackson, the staff, and the players. Pippen was shocked to learn Krause would have traded him to Seattle if the SuperSonics' owner hadn't backed out.

The good news was that Krause signed guard Ron Harper, a proven scorer and disciple of the Triangle. But with all the roster turnover, the team had lost its killer instinct. "Scottie thought the problem was that players were sitting back and waiting for him to perform a miracle, just as they had done with Michael before him," said Jackson. "My reading was that the team didn't have an overwhelming desire to win." [17]

That all changed when Michael Jordan issued a two-word press release: "I'm back." A .200 hitter in the minor leagues, his famous work ethic had not translated to success in a new sport. MLB was heading for a protracted strike when Jordan announced an end to the experiment. "Well," Jackson said when Jordan asked to rejoin the Bulls, "I think we've got a uniform here that might fit you." [18]

When the rumors of his return were confirmed, fans felt a thrill of anticipation on par with learning Santa Claus was not only real but en route to their homes with presents. On March 19, 1995, Jordan was suddenly back on the Bulls for a nationally televised game in Indianapolis. Pacers coach Larry Brown said, "Elvis and the Beatles are back."[19]

Jordan was rusty and the Bulls lost in overtime, but from there Chicago ripped off a 13–3 run as the NBA's ratings spiked. Jordan put up fifty-five points to beat the Knicks in Madison Square Garden. While it appeared that His Airness was well and truly back, Jordan's timing and endurance weren't there yet.

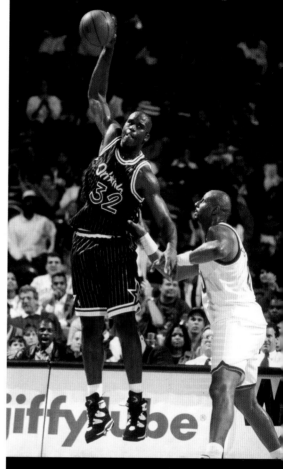

Right from the start of his career Shaquille O'Neal was a force of nature. No one he played against could match "the Diesel's" blend of size, strength, and agility.

There was no question who the team's leader was, however, and it wasn't Jordan. "When Phil said it was time to line up at the start of practice, Jordan would run to be the first one there," remembered newcomer Jud Buechler. "So you'd try and beat him to the line. Then when you see him standing there, looking eye to eye with the coach, hands behind his back, giving Phil total respect … I mean, if the *star* is showing that much respect, are you kidding?"[20]

Meditation and Mindfulness: George Mumford's Influence

A promising basketball player who roomed with Julius Erving at UMass, George Mumford saw his life derailed by alcoholism and heroin addiction. Mumford found help in AA and a detox program, but it was meditation that gave his life new purpose. After studying at UMass's Center for Mindfulness with Jon-Kabat Zinn, author of the bestseller *Wherever You Go, There You Are*, Mumford began helping athletes use these techniques to relieve stress, alleviate the pain of injuries, and improve focus. "There weren't a lot of things that Shaq and Kobe agreed on," said Phil Jackson biographer Roland Lazenby, "but they both agreed on the effectiveness of George Mumford."[21]

Come playoff time, hopes were high. Chicago handled the Charlotte Hornets 3–1 in the first round and faced the young Orlando Magic in the second. The Magic were a tough draw. Not only did they boast already-dominant center Shaquille O'Neal, they had Horace Grant and three deadly long-range shooters.

Jackson concocted an effective defensive strategy, but Chicago's offense floundered. Jordan looked mortal in a Game 1 loss, making uncharacteristic mental errors in the game's final seconds. Jackson put his arm around him. "As many times as we've won behind you, I never expected to see this happen. Let's use it to build a positive. You're our guy, and don't ever forget that."[22]

Jordan bounced back with thirty-eight points in Game 2, a win for Chicago. The squads split the next two games before Grant made his old team pay in Game 5, hitting ten of thirteen shots in a 103–95 win for Orlando. Chicago had no one at the power forward position who could challenge a player like Grant, and it cost them.

"By Game 6 it was clear this version of the Bulls didn't have the deep, intuitive knowledge of each other that a team needs to

> *"Losing is a lens through which you can see yourself more clearly."* [23]
>
> —Phil Jackson

work harmoniously under pressure," said Jackson. "This club didn't have the same 'think power,' to use Michael's phrase, that the championship Bulls had." [24]

In Game 6, Armstrong nailed a three to put Chicago up 102–94 with three and a half minutes left. But the Bulls were out of sync. Their scoring drought spanned seven possessions as the Magic closed the game on a 14–0 run, capped off with a thunderous Shaq dunk that screamed "changing of the guard."

Jackson was haunted by what might have been. Was there anything he could have done differently? "Losing is a lens through which you can see yourself more clearly," he said. A few days later, Jackson's wrestling with what went wrong suddenly yielded a "eureka!" moment. "I could imagine a new incarnation of the Bulls built around the new Michael Jordan, now an elder statesman, not a young, rambunctious warrior." [25] "I couldn't wait to get started," [26] he said.

8

BUILDING A BETTER BULLS TEAM

- - - - - - - - - - - - - - - - - - - -

Phil Jackson met with Michael Jordan soon after the season and asked him if he was coming back. Jordan said he would. "He wasn't happy with how the playoffs had ended," said Jackson. "He had that look in his eye that said, 'I'm going to make somebody pay.'"[1] Jackson promised MJ that the organization would add whatever ingredients were missing and become champions again.

After finishing twelfth in the league in rebounding and getting pushed around by power forwards, the Bulls desperately needed someone to fill Horace Grant's shoes. On the surface, ex-Piston Dennis Rodman didn't seem like the man for the job. While he played superb defense and was a kind of savant at corralling caroms off the rim, his troubled stint in San Antonio led many to view "Dennis the Menace" as an unreliable, unprofessional, and individualistic guy. He seemed like a candidate to produce as many distractions as he did rebounds.

After they talked for several hours, Jackson felt differently about Dennis. "We had connected by our hearts in a nonverbal way, the way of the spirit … I felt assured that he could and would play, and that in the crunch he would do his part."[2] The team did its due diligence and determined that Rodman wasn't a bad guy, just an odd duck. Jordan and Pippen signed off on the trade for their former rival, and the Bulls acquired their X factor, a man the media would add to Chicago's list of superheroes: "Superman, Batman, and Rodman."

Chicago let B. J. Armstrong move on because they had Ron Harper, a much bigger guard who gave Jackson more defensive flexibility. The seven-foot-two (218 cm) Australian Luc Longley would start at center. The team's multifaceted sixth man, Toni Kukoc, kept the second team's offense humming with help from Bill Wennington and Steve Kerr, both of whom excelled at spot-up shooting.

> "[Phil is] a thinker, a compassionate man, a passionate man and a leader from whom there is much to learn."[3]
>
> —Senator Bill Bradley

Rodman's eccentric appearance certainly attracted attention—he had tattoos, piercings, and a series of outlandish hairdos—but he dominated the glass like no one else. His offensive rebounds were

"Quirky" doesn't cover it with Dennis Rodman, but the forward found his calling in "cleaning the glass." Only four players have ever collected more rebounds per minute of game time.

especially valuable because they gave the Bulls second chances to score. Rodman played with a joyful, almost child-like enthusiasm that made him a fan favorite. After every game he'd give his jersey to someone in the crowd. With a sensitive soul and generous nature, he was also an oddly endearing presence off the court.

"Somewhere around the middle of training camp, I realized I was having a lot of fun coaching this team," said Jackson. "And Dennis Rodman brings a lot of levity to the game. I get a kick out of watching him play … There are things about his individuality that remind me of myself."[4] Jackson did notice that when he argued with officials or stalked the sidelines in agitation, Rodman picked up on this energy and mirrored it. Jackson became more peaceful on the bench, to avoid setting off Rodman, and never went back to his more excitable ways.

Jordan entered the 1995–1996 season in phenomenal shape. In the offseason he'd perfected the fade-away jump shot that would become his signature move in this second stint with the Bulls. He was also open to doing less leading by example and more work understanding what made his teammates tick. "It's all about taking responsibility for how you relate to others," mindfulness guru George Mumford told him. "Instead of expecting them to be somewhere else and getting angry and trying to will them to that place, try to meet them where they are and lead them where you want them to go."[5]

On opening night, Jordan scored forty points in a win over Charlotte. In a record-setting 41–3 start, this Bulls team toyed with opponents through two or three quarters before ramping up their pressure defense and blowing them away in the fourth quarter. Pippen had a league-MVP-level year, Rodman blended in perfectly (on the court), and Harper, previously a prolific scorer, accepted (and excelled in) his new role as defensive specialist.

As the Bulls streaked to a 72–10 record, the best in NBA history, they became a traveling road-show some called "the Beatles of basketball," selling out stadiums around the country and garnering breathless local news coverage. Jordan, Pippen, and Rodman were

Lots of Records, But No Ring

With a 73–9 regular season, the 2015–2016 Golden State Warriors broke Chicago's twenty-year-old record. The Warriors also became the first team in NBA history to never lose back-to-back games. Though Steve Kerr was named NBA Coach of the Year, Luke Walton helped the team get off to a 39–4 start while Kerr recovered from back surgery. Steph Curry, Klay Thompson, and Draymond Green were All-Stars and Curry was the first unanimous winner of the league MVP award. However, the 2015–16 Warriors were also the first team to squander a 3–1 lead in the NBA Finals, losing to LeBron James and the Cleveland Cavaliers.

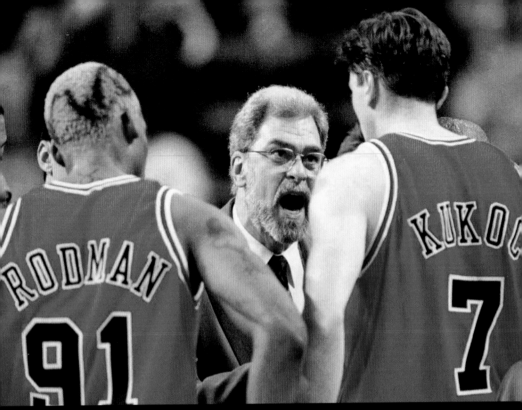

In Game 5 of the 1996 Finals, Jackson knew Toni Kukoc had to adapt his improvisational style to suit the Triangle, but it was a struggle sometimes. Dennis Rodman came up big in Games 2 and 6 (both wins).

swarmed everywhere they went. This was more than a basketball team; it was a cultural phenomenon.

In the first two rounds of the playoffs, the Bulls lost just one game. Then they eagerly confronted the team that had dispatched them the previous year, Orlando. Horace Grant was injured in Game 1 and missed most of the series, contributing to another sweep for Chicago.

Chicago's NBA Finals' foe was a young, athletic Seattle SuperSonics team that played suffocating defense and were fearsome on the fast break. Chicago took the first three games, but losing Ron Harper to injury made the Sonics' offense harder to contain, and Seattle won two in a row on their home floor. Harper's return in Game 6 was a boost for the Bulls' pressure defense, and Rodman came up big, controlling the glass with nineteen rebounds (eleven offensive) and scoring on key put-backs. Kukoc was money from three-point land. Jordan dedicated the 83–75 win, which came on Father's Day, to James Jordan. He cried after every championship, but this time his tears were bittersweet.

Chicago won eighty-seven of the hundred games they played that year. Jordan led the league in scoring again, and Jackson was named Coach of the Year. The only question after such an incredible season: how on Earth could they top it?

RESILIENT ENOUGH TO REPEAT?

The team opened the 1996–97 season 12–0, an even better start than the year before. Jordan dropped fifty on the Heat in their third game. His turn-around jumper was now virtually unstoppable. Rodman, however, was losing focus, and Jackson theorized he suffered from ADHD. Dennis said he was bored with basketball and his play reflected it, culminating in Chicago suspending him for two games after he was ejected from a game in Toronto. Then, in January, the league suspended him for eleven games after he kicked a courtside cameraman in the groin. Jackson didn't have to get explicit with Rodman to send the message that he was on thin ice—with everyone. "My tactic was to hold him accountable for his actions the same way I did everyone else," said Jackson. "He seemed to appreciate this. Once, he told reporters that what he liked about me was that I treated him 'like a man.'"[6]

Jackson's approach to coaching the team was to let them make mistakes and work their way out of difficult situations on the court. "He can sit there and let more bad things go on in the course of a ballgame than any coach I've ever been associated with, or known,"[7] said Tex Winter. But no error went unexamined for long. Phil discussed the players' performance the next day: in practice, video review, or individual meetings. When he was critical, he often made light of it, such as intercutting Three Stooges clips into game-film of dumb plays. He wouldn't embarrass individuals in front of the group.

At 69–13, the Bulls finished a couple of games off the prior season's pace, and questions about the future threatened their peace of mind. Jackson, Jordan, and Rodman were all on one-year contracts. "He's very good at handling distractions," Winter said of Jackson. "He says, 'We're just playing this thing out. Let's worry about today. Don't worry about tomorrow.'"[8]

Movies with a Message

When preparing game tape to review with his team, Phil would often edit in movie scenes to make points he'd rather not spell out verbally. "Phil does a lot of stuff that if you just let it pass, you don't really understand," said Bill Wennington. "But if you think about it, he's trying to get us motivated or thinking at a deeper level. Sometimes we catch on, and sometimes we don't."[9] Later, Kobe Bryant said, "I like to try to figure out what Phil was actually thinking when he put the clip in there. All the messages he has … Some clips are funny. Some are to be taken a little more seriously."[10]

In the playoffs Michael took the lead, which worked well enough against Washington, but then Atlanta handed Chicago its first home defeat in the last two postseasons. Jordan eased off on his aggressiveness, and Rodman had a strong outing in the decisive Game 5.

Chicago proceeded to the conference finals, where they'd play Jackson's old pal Pat Riley and the Miami Heat. (An upset loss in the 1996 regular season prompted Jackson to tell his players, "Never lose to that guy."[11]) After two ugly, low-scoring wins, Jackson tweaked the Triangle to open up the offense, and Riley had no answer for it; Game 3 was a blowout for the Bulls. Winter later called it one of Jackson's finest coaching exhibitions. While Miami got Game 4, Jordan was on fire, and it carried over into the clincher, as did Rodman's renewed effort on both sides of the floor. "They are the greatest team since the Celtics won eleven in thirteen years," Riley told reporters after the 100–87 Bulls win. "I don't think anybody's going to win again until Michael retires."[12]

In the previous season's Western Conference Finals, the Utah Jazz lost to Seattle in seven games. This year they made it through and

> *"The Mailman doesn't deliver on Sunday."*
>
> —Scottie Pippen

presented Chicago with a new challenge. Utah's duo of John Stockton and Karl "the Mailman" Malone was the league's best point guard/ power forward pairing in recent memory. They ran the pick-and-roll to perfection. Stockton was both the quintessential passer and a dangerous shooter, while Malone had just won the league MVP award.

Jordan and Jackson show off their hardware (NBA Finals MVP and Larry O'Brien Trophy) after completing their second three-peat together, a joyous final note in "the Last Dance."

Game 1 was a back-and-forth affair featuring heroics on both sides. With barely a minute left in the game, Pippen and Stockton buried threes, and Jordan clanked a free throw. The game was tied when Rodman fouled Malone, and Pippen whispered to Malone, "The Mailman doesn't deliver on Sunday." Malone missed both free throws, and Jordan fired in the game-winner, a twenty-footer, as the clock hit double zero. Chicago cruised in Game 2, but, at altitude in Salt Lake City, the Bulls faltered in Game 3. Malone scored thirty-seven in a 104–93 pounding. Game 4 was a thriller, but down the stretch Chicago couldn't buy a basket. With seventeen seconds left, Karl cashed in on his free throws and Utah tied the series.

The pivotal Game 5 became known as "The Flu Game," one of Michael Jordan's greatest moments. A famous image of Pippen (literally) supporting his sick teammate doesn't fully convey how ill Jordan was in the early morning that day. But he scored thirty-eight in a backbreaking Bulls win. "He hadn't gotten out of bed all day," said Jackson. "Standing up was literally a nauseating experience, and he had dizzy spells."[13] Pippen told MJ to conserve all of his energy for offense; orchestrating the defense was Pippen's problem. This made Jordan's performance possible.

In Game 6, Jordan put in another thirty-nine points, but Kerr got to be the hero, hitting a three-pointer (on Jordan's assist) to break a tie with five seconds left. Afterwards, Jordan wanted to share his Finals MVP honors with Pippen. "I'll take the trophy," he said, "But I'm going to give Scottie the car. He deserves it as much as I did."[14] Jackson's tribe reigned supreme once again.

9

FAREWELLS AND GREETINGS

- - - - - - - - - - - - - - - -

The Chicago dynasty was doomed, even if the team went 82–0 in 1997–98. Years of conflict bubbling under the surface between "management" (owner Jerry Reinsdorf and GM Jerry Krause) and the "team" (Phil Jackson, his coaches, and his players) could no longer be repressed. The team felt management begrudged them every penny of their salaries, viewing contract negotiations as a game to be won or lost. Even Michael Jordan was hurt when Reinsdorf said, "I might live to regret this" after agreeing to pay him $30 million for the 1996–97 season.

After another round of adversarial contract negotiations, the nucleus of the team returned for one more go-round. Krause made it abundantly clear, publicly and personally, that this would be Phil Jackson's final year as coach of the Chicago Bulls. Jordan made it clear that if Jackson left, he would retire.

Jackson dubbed the season "the Last Dance" (T-shirts were printed), and his feelings were mixed. "The finality of it gave the season a certain resonance that bonded the team closely together," he said. "It felt as if we were on a sacred mission, driven by a force that went beyond fame, glory, and all the other spoils of victory. We were doing this one for the pure joy of playing together one more time. It felt magical."[1]

Pippen missed the first two months of the season with an injury, and, not surprisingly, the Bulls got off to a slow start in their last rodeo. When Pippen returned, the Bulls finished the season in typically sensational fashion. The only black mark on their record was an overtime loss in Dallas that delivered home-court advantage to the Jazz.

Undeterred, the Bulls swept their first round opponent for the third year in a row. They lost just one game in the second round. At thirty-five, Jordan became the NBA's oldest player to win MVP. Jackson gathered the players, coaches, and training staff in the "tribal room" to share a paragraph they'd written about what the season, and the team, meant to them. After everyone spoke, they put their words in a coffee can. Jackson turned out the lights and burned their messages. Everyone sat in silence until the flames died down. "I don't think the bond among us had ever been stronger,"[2] said Jackson.

The team's train to their final Finals nearly derailed against Indiana. Against the backdrop of dueling interviews from Jordan and Reinsdorf, the organization's togetherness (if not the team's) was at an all-time low. Led by the spectacular shooting of Reggie Miller, the Pacers mounted two impressive comebacks to tie the series at two games apiece. Back in Chicago, the Bulls routed their opponents in Game 5, but Indiana answered in Game 6 with more late-game heroics. This series was going the distance. Even Jordan felt less comfortable in Game 7, knowing anything could happen and there was no margin for error. "We could lose this game," Jackson told the team, "But what's important is playing with the right kind of effort, and not being overtaken by the fear of losing."[3]

Even on their home court, the Bulls found themselves in an early hole. With Jordan off his game, Jackson called on his bench, trusting Kerr and Buechler to provide buckets and hustle, respectively. Kukoc took over in the third quarter and staked Chicago to a 69–65 lead at the start of the fourth quarter. Jordan's jumpers wouldn't go in, but his free throws did, and Chicago won 88–83.

Opening their Finals rematch in Utah, Chicago lost in overtime. Jordan's relapse into singlehanded scoring binges almost cost them a win in Game 2, but Chicago managed to wrest away Utah's home-court advantage. Back home, the Bulls thumped the Jazz in Game 3, 96–54. It was a record margin. Rodman hit four free throws in the closing seconds of Game 4 to give the Bulls a 3–1 lead in the series. He generally missed about half of his free throws, so this was a clutch performance.

> *"Love is the force that ignites the spirit and binds teams together."*[4]
>
> —Phil Jackson

The Bulls didn't show killer instinct in Game 5, and headed back to Utah after Jordan missed what would have been a game-winning three. Back spasms limited Pippen's minutes in Game 6 but Jordan picked up the slack, scoring forty-five in his final game as a Bull. With Utah's 86–83 lead, Jackson called timeout. The play went to Jordan, who scored. Then he got a steal and took the ball upcourt. To punctuate his performance, and his career, MJ swished the game-winner. After the final buzzer, Jackson hugged him. "Even though Michael would return to basketball years later to play for the Washington Wizards, this is the shot everyone thinks of as his final bow," said Jackson. "A perfect ending if ever there was one."[5]

Jordan said the team needed Jackson more than ever in their second three-peat. "In the first run [of championships], the egos hadn't set in yet. But in the second run, we had a lot of different personalities to mesh together, and the egos were really strong. Phil had to bring us together as a brotherhood."[6]

"The first series of championships transformed the Bulls from an 'I'm great, you're not' team to a 'We're great, they're not' team,'" said Jackson. "But for the second series, the team adopted a broader 'Life is great' point of view. By midseason it became clear to me

The Phil Jackson Book Club

Phil Jackson liked to share the lessons he learned from great books and send messages to his players about what they needed to work on. So it became a tradition for him to give each player a hand-picked book to read, often before a long road trip. Though his choices seemed calculated, the intent was never obvious, and he never explained further. Nor did he force players to read the books he gave them (a good thing, because Michael Jordan and Kobe Bryant rarely did).

that it wasn't competition per se that was driving the team; it was simply the joy of the game itself."[7]

The inevitable breakup happened. Reinsdorf made overtures to Jackson after the season, but by then Jackson was at peace with moving on. After a year away from the game to recharge his batteries, the beginning of Jackson's tenure with the Los Angeles Lakers sadly coincided with the dissolution of his marriage to June. He acknowledged being too consumed with basketball to be the husband she deserved, and the decision to start over with another team was the final straw that led the couple to separate. They remain good friends. "She wants to get out of the shadow of being an NBA wife,"[8] said Jackson. "I still overextend myself in an effort to please too many people at the expense of my loved ones."[9]

COULD THE STARS SHINE TOGETHER?

The Lakers were the perfect reclamation project for Jackson. They had lost in the playoffs three years in a row. It seemed more a matter of the mind than physical ability. As Jackson wrote in *Eleven Rings*, "The team was loaded with talent, including rising stars Shaquille O'Neal and Kobe Bryant. But the Lakers had struggled in the playoffs because of weak group chemistry, and the players lacked the mental toughness to finish off big games."[10]

Jackson set about transforming another *me* team into a *we* team. The Lakers were fragmented, and the toxic relationship of their two superstars, Shaq and Kobe, threatened to tear them apart. Shaq was

Before Jackson arrived in L.A., Shaq and Kobe butted heads constantly. He was able to negotiate a truce that was very, very good while it lasted.

a fun-loving, easy-going guy and Kobe was a killer in the Jordan mold; his intense focus and bitingly sarcastic nature rubbed Shaq the wrong way.

What's more, ten years after taking over the Bulls, Jackson found the Lakers had shorter attention spans and had come up in a basketball culture that "reinforces egoistic behavior," he said. "As they grow older and continue to succeed, they become surrounded by legions of agents, promoters, groupies, and other sycophants who keep telling them they're 'da man … ' What's more, L.A. is a world devoted to celebrating the notion of the glorified self." [11]

Jackson brought in his former Bulls assistant coaches Jim Cleamons, Frank Hamblen, and Tex Winter. He also asked psychologist George Mumford to install meditation practices. Kobe loved it. "Working with George helps us get issues out of the way before they even start," said Bryant. The meditation ramped up from three minutes to ten and players' concentration improved to the point that they could review entire game tapes with full attention. "The constant practice of awareness and concentration certainly made the guys easier to coach,"[12] said Jackson.

That wasn't all Jackson did to enhance the mental strength of his new team. "I also introduced the players to yoga, tai chi, and other Eastern practices to help them balance mind, body, and spirit. In Chicago we'd used meditation primarily to increase awareness on the court. But with this team our goal was to bond the players together so they would experience what we called 'one breath, one mind.'" His aim was to teach the players that the panic they felt under pressure, in the playoffs, would become inner peace if they trusted in their interconnectedness. "That's what gives you strength and energy in the midst of chaos."[13]

The Triangle was perfect for Shaq, a center who was vastly more physically talented than any player in that position Jackson had coached in Chicago. Kobe reminded him of a young Michael Jordan in more ways than one. Though no one worked harder, the twenty-one-year-old had the same instinct to abandon the system and take matters into his own hands. "His selfish mistakes were hurting the team," said Jackson. "I also indicated to him that if he didn't want to share the ball with his teammates, I would gladly work out a trade for him. I had no trouble being the bad cop in this situation."[14] Point guard Derek Fisher said that Jackson gave Kobe time to breathe before telling him what needed to change, and didn't single him out. "It was never as if Kobe was the only guy on the team who needed to make adjustments, or to improve in certain areas."[15]

Years later, Kobe would reflect on how much he grew to appreciate Jackson's hokey old offense, the Triangle. "The opposition didn't know what we were going to do," said Bryant. "Why? Because *we* didn't know what we were going to do from moment to moment. Everybody was reading and reacting to each other. It was a great orchestra."[16]

Jackson and Jeanie Buss, the Lakers' team executive VP of business operations, began a discreet relationship that sent the tabloids into overdrive. Jeanie was the owner's daughter, but she was also a smart, savvy businesswoman with a great sense of humor. "During the twelve or so years that he coached the Lakers, I really got into the role of team mom," said Buss. "I got to see another side of basketball that I hadn't seen—that what Phil tries to create is a family."[17]

The 1999–2000 season saw Los Angeles post the NBA's best record, 67–15. Jackson's vision for Shaq thriving in the Triangle was realized: O'Neal led the league in scoring and was named MVP of the

> *"What makes basketball so exhilarating is the joy of losing yourself completely in the dance, even if it's just for one beautiful, transcendent moment."*[18]
>
> —Phil Jackson

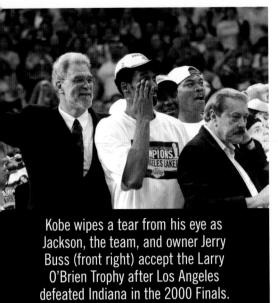

Kobe wipes a tear from his eye as Jackson, the team, and owner Jerry Buss (front right) accept the Larry O'Brien Trophy after Los Angeles defeated Indiana in the 2000 Finals.

league. That first year, Jackson focused his energy on the Hulk-sized center, from whom he wanted more leadership, conditioning, and defense. The deal was that if Shaq fulfilled his obligations, he'd be the centerpiece of the offense. There was no star-coddling. As reserve forward Rick Fox explained, "He's gone as hard at guys as I've seen anybody go at someone … He's pushing buttons to make sure guys continually come to work, step their games up and get better."[19]

In the playoffs, the Lakers reached the Western Conference Finals, where Pippen and his new team, the Portland Trail Blazers, put up quite a fight. Pippen knew how to defend the Triangle, and he could still score, too. The series went seven games. In the deciding game, Jackson called timeout with L.A. down sixteen points. He convinced Shaq to concentrate on defense, while challenging the others to make shots when the Blazers' D collapsed on "the Big Aristotle." The team's investment in the mental game paid off, as Shaq stayed focused and positive, and his teammates took their cues from him. "I don't think our players played with a lot of pressure on them,"[20] Jackson said.

The Lakers completed a historic fourth-quarter comeback with defense, a critical Kobe to Shaq pass, and the Diesel's rim-rattling dunk, which sealed the Lakers' win. "They had worked out a mutually agreeable way to collaborate that culminated in this dramatic closeout shot," said Jackson. "That moment was an important turning point for our team."[21]

The Lakers then bested the Pacers in six games to win the NBA Finals. The most notable thing about the series, for Jackson, was that Kobe played Game 4 with an excruciatingly painful ankle injury and still scored half of the team's sixteen points in overtime, after Shaq fouled out. The result was a 120–118 win. Kobe's hard-fought performance reminded Jackson of Bryant's idol, Michael Jordan. "It was gratifying to see that the basic principles we'd developed with the Bulls could be so effective in transforming a very different kind of team into champions," Jackson said later. "Obviously, Shaq's dominance was a key factory in our victory, and so was Kobe's relentless creativity. But what pleased me even more was the synergy the two of them exhibited in the last part of the season, after they realized they needed each other to achieve the only goal that mattered."[22]

Basketball Is in Her Blood

As a nineteen-year-old student at USC, Jeanie Buss became the general manager of her family's professional tennis team, the Los Angeles Strings. She later became the president of the Great Western Forum, the Lakers' arena until Staples Center opened in 1999. Jeanie's father, Dr. Jerry Buss, the Lakers' owner since 1979, instructed that upon his passing ownership of the franchise be divided among his six children. Jeanie ultimately became the controlling owner and president. After four straight losing seasons, she fired her brother, Jim Buss, in 2017 and hired Magic Johnson as the Lakers' president of basketball operations.

A HOLLYWOOD ENDING

- -

O ver the summer Kobe Bryant took his still-developing skills to another level, and he inflicted his new greatness on the rest of the league in the 2000–2001 season. "By default the role of orchestrator on the Lakers fell to Kobe, but he wasn't interested in becoming Shaq's Pippen," said Jackson. "He wanted to create shots for himself."[1]

Rick Fox compared Kobe to Michael Jordan, with whom he'd worked as a college student. The parallels went beyond a desire to "take the shot" themselves. "To them, winning is all that matters. And they demand that everyone around them act the same way, regardless of whether they can or not. They say, 'Find somewhere inside yourself to get better, because that's what I'm doing every minute of the day.' They have no tolerance for anything less. None."[2]

The Kobe and Shaq feud escalated that year, but Jackson took a page from the playbook of, of all people, Jerry Reinsdorf. "He once said that the best way to handle flare-ups is to sleep on them. The point is to avoid acting out of anger and creating an even stickier mess."[3] He also knew that Kobe would let him push him harder than Shaq would, and Shaq would appreciate Jackson doing that. So he gave the younger player strong direction on how to mature and grow.

That season had the happiest of endings. The team peaked in a way that even the Bulls had not, rampaging through the playoffs with a remarkable 15–1 record and a Larry O'Brien trophy. But more importantly to Jackson, under pressure they had the calm and composure of the Bulls. Kobe was transcendent and Shaq, far from being jealous, said, "I think he's the best player in the league—by far. When he's playing like that, scoring, getting everybody involved, playing good defense, there's nothing you can say."[4]

"The mistake that championship teams often make is to try to repeat their winning formula," said Jackson. "But that rarely works because by the time the next season starts, your opponents have figured out how to counter every move you made. The key to sustained success is to keep growing as a team."[5]

The 2001–02 team got off to a start that had observers wondering if they'd break the Bulls' record for wins, but the Lakers cooled off as inconsistency plagued them. They generally beat the best teams but lost to teams they shouldn't have. Yet, in the playoffs, Jackson's troops began to play like champions. It was a good thing, too, because their division rivals, the Sacramento Kings, had home-court in the Western finals. The heated adversaries split the series' first two games before Kings Chris Webber and Mike Bibby combined for fifty in a Sacramento win. "Well, we're not bored now,"[6] joked Kobe.

In the next game, L.A.'s Robert Horry earned the nickname "Big Shot Rob" when he unleashed a three-point attempt at the buzzer and it found nothing but net, completing a twenty-point comeback. But Sacramento took Game 5 at home to pull ahead, 3–2.

> *"The key to sustained success is to keep growing as a team."*[1]
>
> —Phil Jackson

Three days later Shaq came out with a vengeance, owning the paint with forty-one points and seventeen rebounds. Kobe chipped in thirty-one and hit four critical foul shots in the final seconds to secure a 106–100 victory.

Game 7 was in the state capital, where the "Beat L.A.!" chants were always deafening. "This was an excellent road team, but playing a seventh game on an opponent's court is the most drop-dead-challenging test," said Jackson. To combat the inevitable attack of nerves, he organized a pregame meditation session at the hotel. "As we sat in silence, I could sense that the players were pulling themselves together, preparing mentally for the showdown that awaited them."[8]

The game was a classic. Seventeen lead changes across three hours of play stretched into overtime. But the Lakers' mental fortitude showed when they pulled off a twenty-seven of thirty-three performance at the free-throw line. Los Angeles controlled the extra period and emerged with a hard-fought 112–106 win. All five starters finished the game with ten or more points, a sign of the Triangle in action. After that, winning the NBA Finals seemed easy, as the peaking Lakers rolled over the New Jersey Nets 4–0.

After an early exit (for them) in the 2002–03 postseason, Jackson's team returned to the NBA Finals with additions Karl Malone and Gary Payton. But this season revealed their fragile chemistry. Kobe had been arrested on rape charges and was jetting back and forth from Colorado for pretrial hearings. (Charges were dropped after the season, and the civil suit against Bryant ended in a settlement.) Though Jackson found it hard to believe that Kobe was capable of committing such a crime, the case changed his perception of his star. They had basketball conflicts, as well. "I wanted him to stop being the lone ranger and come into the group, as a leader, but he had his own problems to deal with,"[9] said Jackson. Though their relationship suffered greatly, the tension was nothing compared to the animosity building between Kobe and Shaq. Their truce had evaporated, replaced by open and public sniping in the media.

"Managing anger is every coach's most difficult task," said Jackson. "It requires a great deal of patience and finesse because the line between the aggressive intensity needed to win games and destructive anger is often razor thin."[10]

Fisher Put His Family First

In 1996, Derek Fisher and Kobe Bryant were rookies with the Lakers, though "Fish" was four years older. The University of Arkansas at Little Rock product was considerably less heralded than his teammate, who made the leap to the NBA from Lower Merion High School. In 2007, Fisher walked away from a large contract with the Utah Jazz to return to Los Angeles, where his ten-month-old daughter Tatum could get the best possible treatment for her rare form of cancer. Today the chances of the cancer returning are remote.

Jackson and Kobe had a heart-to-heart after the All-Star Break that began to heal their rift. Jackson offered the advice that basketball could become a refuge from Bryant's other woes, as it was for Michael Jordan. That meeting laid the groundwork for a much healthier coach/player relationship down the road.

A string of injuries greatly limited the Lakers' star-studded line-up's time on the court together, but they entered the playoffs as the number-two seed in the West. Still, in the second round San Antonio jumped out to a 2–0 series lead. The Lakers stormed back to tie the series entering Game 5. They got up by sixteen points in the third quarter, but it was the Spurs' turn to mount a thrilling comeback. Tim Duncan hit a miraculous shot to give his team the lead with less than half a second left on the clock. Jackson assured the Lakers that they were going to win. Payton found Derek Fisher for a shot he got off at the last possible nanosecond. It went in, causing bedlam back home in Los Angeles and giving the guard a revered place in Laker lore.

For the first time in his career, however, Jackson would lose in the NBA Finals. The Detroit Pistons were too athletic, energetic, and cohesive for the Lakers' collection of mostly aging veterans. "My biggest disappointment during this season was our inability to shut out all the distractions and mold this talented group of superstars into the powerhouse it should have been,"[11] said the coach.

ENCORE IN L.A.

Almost everyone parted ways after that tumultuous season, and the Lakers missed the playoffs in 2004–05. Jackson traveled the world and rode his motorcycle. Jeanie Buss asked him to coach the team again, and the idea of rebuilding from scratch appealed to him. More importantly, he still felt the drive to win. "I'm not sure that I'm capable of living a life that lacks a basic level of competition,"[12] he admitted.

A return would be impossible if Jackson couldn't rebuild his relationship with Kobe. Shaq had been shipped to Miami (where he'd win another ring), and the "Black Mamba" had signed a long-term deal with the Lakers. It was Kobe's team now. In Jackson's 2004 book *The Last Season*, he called Kobe "uncoachable." But nothing he put on the record about Kobe was too harsh to be called constructive criticism. Both parties agreed to forgive and forget.

Upon learning that Jackson was back with the Lakers, Shaq said, "I thank him for taking me to a level I couldn't get to myself. I wish him the best of luck. He'll need it."[13]

The puzzle pieces necessary to form a championship portrait were not in place for the 2005–06 Lakers. Or the 2006–07 team, for that matter. Both were bounced in the first round of the playoffs. No one thought these thin rosters underachieved, though Kobe had taken his scoring to the stratosphere. Most notably, he tallied eighty-one points in a win over Toronto, second only to Wilt Chamberlain's legendary one-hundred-point game. On that occasion, Jackson was proud of his pupil. "On this night, it was Kobe who was responsible for the team's success. Without his heroic performance, we would have lost. His outburst came in the context of the game. I trusted him, and he trusted me."[14]

Though coach and player were now getting along, Bryant was so upset with the state of the Lakers' personnel he demanded a trade—it was his only leverage to make something happen. Jackson agreed that changes needed to be made. "I was reminded of how important character is when it comes to winning big games," he said. "What this team needed was more heart."[15]

Lakers GM Mitch Kupchak made the right moves for the 2007–08 season, beginning with re-signing Derek Fisher. "Fish" was a gritty, tough-minded leader unafraid to hoist a shot with everything on the line. Fisher was one of Kobe's best friends in basketball, so his return would calm troubled waters.

Then Kupchak traded for Trevor Ariza, a quick, well-rounded swingman, and All-Star Pau Gasol, a standout on Spain's Olympic team. The forward/center had a keen intellect and a game that blended size and finesse. His addition allowed Lamar Odom to become the third option on offense, a role that allowed the silky-smooth big man to thrive. Gasol would prove to be the most important addition to one of Jackson's teams since Dennis Rodman. Bryant and Gasol became a powerful one-two punch. As Jackson remembered it, "As

The Rivalry That Riveted America

The greatest rivalry in NBA history is that between the Boston Celtics and Los Angeles Lakers. Since 1959, the teams have met with the championship on the line a record twelve times. The first eight showdowns ended in heartbreak for L.A., but since then Boston has lost three out of four. The intrigue peaked in the 1980s, when Magic Johnson (Lakers) and Larry Bird (Celtics) had three head-to-head matchups in the Finals. Pitting an East Coast, hard-nosed style of ball against the West Coast's flashy "Showtime," these clashes caused interest in the NBA to skyrocket.

Jackson and an emotional Derek Fisher reflect on their journey together after the Lakers survived the Celtics' onslaught in the 2010 Finals. During his career, Fisher was directly involved in several improbable playoff wins.

soon as he arrived, we transformed from a team struggling to eke out one hundred points a game to a fast-paced scoring machine, averaging 110-plus and having a lot more fun doing it."[16]

This was the right combination to go far in the playoffs. In the Conference Finals, the Lakers lost just one game to the defending champion Spurs. Kobe was voted league MVP. Though Los Angeles entered the championship round with high hopes, a special Boston Celtics team dismantled the still-gelling group from La La Land. "There's nothing like a humiliating loss to focus the mind,"[17] said Jackson.

The 2008–09 team returned with fire in their eyes and meshed like few had before. "There wasn't anything that was going to hold us back," said Fisher. "No matter what we faced, no matter how many ups and downs, we knew we were tough enough—mentally and physically—to figure this out. And we did." [18] A key factor was Kobe's maturing as a team leader, as Jordan had before him.

At 65–17, this group posted the third best record in the Lakers' illustrious history. "This was not the most talented team I'd ever coached, nor the

> *"Leadership is not about forcing your will on others. It's about mastering the art of letting go."* [19]
> —Phil Jackson

most physically dominant," said Jackson. "But the players had a

One of the greatest big-game players of all time, Kobe Bryant had a Jordanesque ability to rise to the occasion when his team needed a nearly superhuman effort to win.

deep spiritual connection that allowed them, every now and then, to perform miracles on the court." [20] Balanced scoring and lockdown defense, signatures of a Phil Jackson team, saw them through the playoff field. Though Houston took them to seven games and Denver six, L.A. dispatched Orlando 4–1 to win the NBA championship and break Jackson's tie with Boston's Red Auerbach for most titles as a coach (ten). Fisher was the hero in Game 4, but Kobe took charge in the deciding game. "The look of pride and joy in Kobe's eyes made all the pain we'd endured in our journey together worth it,"[21] said Jackson.

The next year the Lakers added Ron Artest, a Rodman-esque character well suited for the team's NBA Finals opponents. The Boston Celtics were back, and they played a style of ball Jackson publicly characterized as "roughhouse." Powered by Ray Allen's eight long-range bombs, Boston left Los Angeles with a split. In Game 3, Fisher shut down the Celtics' top shooter and hit five field goals of his own in the fourth quarter to help L.A. win. But Boston tied it right back up again and moved ahead after Game 5. Then the Lakers' defense, and Pau Gasol's near-triple double, were the difference in a win that set the table for another climactic Game 7.

Before the game, Jackson led the team in their longest meditation of the season. Kobe came out firing, and missing. Boston was up by thirteen in the third quarter when Jackson called timeout to settle down his team. From there, the Lakers crept closer and trailed 57–53 entering the final period. Fisher tied the game with a three, and Kobe added another. With 1:30 left in regulation, the teams traded trifectas before the psychologically centered Lakers hit their free throws to eke out an 83–79 win. Jackson's ex-wife June attended the postgame celebration of the Lakers' sixteenth NBA championship and Jackson's thirteenth (the first two were won as a player). "For me, this was the most gratifying victory of my career,"[22] said Jackson.

There would be no third three-peat for Phil Jackson in what would
be his final season coaching the Lakers. Something was off about the
2010–11 team, and it wasn't just Kobe's knee injuries. Free agency
had sapped the team's depth, and a new defensive system didn't click.
Fatigue, personal issues, the immaturity of some of their players,
and, of course, the talent of their opponents added up to the end of
an era. "I've never had one of my teams fall apart in such a strange
and spooky way before,"[23] said Jackson of the Lakers' second-round
elimination at the hands of the Dallas Mavericks.

Much as the world does not remember Michael Jordan for his baseball career, and Phil Jackson's next position as a team executive with

In 2014, Phil Jackson returned to the team, and the city, where his NBA
odyssey began. In June 2017, he left the organization after years of fraught personnel decisions. Jackson is known better as a coach than an executive, and currently
holds the record for highest win percentage of any coach in the NBA Hall of Fame.

the Knicks may be better forgotten. Jackson lasted three turbulent seasons as team president (2014–2017). Though his tenure produced the prodigious Kristaps Porziņģis, his best draft pick's displeasure with the direction of the team (and Jackson putting Porziņģis on the trade block) led directly to Jackson's dismissal.

It seems clear that Jackson is best suited to work as coach, mentor, and guide. His biographer Peter Richmond wrote, "He was a teacher, and is there ever a higher compliment we can bestow? Skim the later-life résumés of the Kerrs, the Paxsons and countless others. They found happiness and success after playing for Phil." Richmond adds, "Phil Jackson is the greatest coach in not just NBA history but professional sports history … If you're going to live your life based on sport's adherence to statistics, the numbers say there's Phil Jackson, and then there's everyone else."[24]

Whatever is next for Phil Jackson, he has achieved a sports immortality unlike anyone else. That must be gratifying for a man whose spirituality is largely based on seeing the value of our connection to other souls. And, of course, our connection to the moment we are living *right now.* "For me, basketball is an expression of life, a single, sometimes glittering thread, that reflects the whole," said Jackson. "Like life, basketball is messy and unpredictable. It has its way with you, no matter how hard you try to control it. The trick is to experience each moment with a clear mind and open heart. When you do that, the game—and life—will take care of itself."[25]

CHRONOLOGY

1945 Philip Douglas Jackson is born in Deer Lodge, Montana.

1967 In the second round of the NBA Draft, the New York Knicks select Jackson, a power forward from the University of North Dakota.

1970 The Knicks defeat the Los Angeles Lakers to win their first NBA championship, though an injured Jackson is not on the active roster.

1973 Jackson contributes to New York's second NBA title, another win over the Los Angeles Lakers.

1980 After two seasons with the New Jersey Nets, Jackson's career as a player comes to an end.

1984 Jackson leads the Albany Patroons to a league championship.

1987 The Chicago Bulls hire Jackson as an assistant coach.

1989 After the dismissal of Doug Collins, Chicago elevates Jackson to head coach.

1991 The Bulls defeat the Lakers to win the franchise's first NBA championship.

1992 Chicago goes "back-to-back" with their NBA Finals win over the Portland Trail Blazers.

1993 Chicago completes a "three-peat" by beating the Phoenix Suns.

1996 After the return of Michael Jordan and the addition of Dennis Rodman, the Bulls defeat the Seattle SuperSonics to claim their fourth championship. Jackson is voted NBA Coach of the Year.

1997 Chicago bests Utah in six games to win another NBA title.

1998 In an NBA Finals rematch, the Bulls again top the Jazz to give Jackson his sixth championship as a coach.

2000 Jackson's new team, the Los Angeles Lakers, outlasts the Indiana Pacers to win the championship in six games.

2001 The Lakers defeat the Philadelphia 76ers to successfully defend their title.

2002 Jackson pulls off a second "three-peat" as Los Angeles sweeps the New Jersey Nets for Jackson's ninth NBA championship.

2004 A star-studded Lakers roster fails in the NBA Finals, losing to an inspired Detroit Pistons team.

2007 Jackson is inducted into the Basketball Hall of Fame.

2008 After a hiatus, Jackson again leads the Lakers to the Finals, only to lose to the Boston Celtics in five games.

2009 Los Angeles defeats Orlando in the Finals, winning the series 4–1. With his tenth NBA championship, Jackson breaks Red Auerbach's record for coach with the most titles in NBA history.

2010 For the fourth time in his career, Jackson presides over back-to-back championship as Los Angeles avenges 2008's defeat by winning a seven-game series against Boston.

2017 After three unsuccessful seasons as Knicks' team president, Jackson is let go.

CHAPTER NOTES

- - - - - - - - - - - - - - - -

INTRODUCTION

1. Phil Jackson and Charley Rosen, *Sacred Hoops* (New York, NY: Hyperion, 1995), p. 92.
2. Jackson and Rosen, *Sacred Hoops,* p. 163.
3. Phil Jackson and Hugh Delehanty, *Eleven Rings: The Soul of Success* (New York, NY: The Penguin Press, 2013), p. 94.
4. Alex Belth, "The Secret of Phil Jackson's Success: He Never Stopped Questioning," Deadspin, December 27, 2013, https://thestacks.deadspin.com/what-made-phil-jackson-a-great-coach-1489932960.
5. Peter Richmond, *Lord of the Rings* (New York, NY: Penguin Group, 2013), p. 328.

CHAPTER 1. THE JOURNEY BEGINS

1. Phil Jackson and Hugh Delehanty, *Eleven Rings: The Soul of Success* (New York, NY: The Penguin Press, 2013), p. 46.
2. Mike Sager, "Phil Jackson: What I've Learned," *Esquire*, May 8, 2011, http://www.esquire.com/sports/interviews/a4112/phil-jackson-0208.

3. Phil Jackson and Charles Rosen, *Maverick* (Chicago, IL: Playboy Press, 1975), p. 17.

4. Phil Jackson and Charley Rosen, *More Than a Game* (New York, NY: Seven Stories Press, 2001), p. 20.

5. Jackson and Rosen, *Maverick*, p. 18.

6. Jackson and Delehanty, p. 47.

7. Peter Richmond, *Lord of the Rings* (New York, NY: Penguin Group, 2013), p. 25.

8. Richmond, p. 23.

9. Ibid.

10. Richmond, p. 25.

11. Jackson and Rosen, *More Than a Game*, p. 30.

12. Jackson and Rosen, *Maverick*, p. 2.

13. Jackson and Rosen, *More Than a Game*, p. 40.

CHAPTER 2. THE PURITY OF UNSELFISH PLAY

1. Phil Jackson and Charles Rosen, *Maverick* (Chicago, IL: Playboy Press, 1975), p. 3.

2. Peter Richmond, *Lord of the Rings* (New York, NY: Penguin Group, 2013), p. 61.

3. Phil Jackson and Charley Rosen, *More Than a Game* (New York, NY: Seven Stories Press, 2001), p. 39.

4. Richmond, p. 79.

5. Phil Jackson and Hugh Delehanty, *Eleven Rings: The Soul of Success* (New York, NY: The Penguin Press, 2013), p. 37.

6. Sam Goldaper, "Knicks' Quiet Leader William (Red) Holzman," *New York Times*, May 12, 1973, http://www.nytimes.com/1973/05/12/archives/knicks-quiet-leader-william-red-holzman.html.

7. Richmond, p. 54.

8. Jackson and Delehanty, p. 42.

9. Jackson and Delehanty, p. 31.

10. Jackson and Delehanty, p. 26.

11. Phil Jackson and Charley Rosen, *Sacred Hoops* (New York, NY: Hyperion, 1995), p. 41.

12. Richmond, p. 79.

13. Richmond, p. 81.

14. Jackson and Rosen, *More Than a Game*, p. 50.

15. Richmond, p. 86.

CHAPTER 3. A VAGABOND COACH

1. Peter Richmond, *Lord of the Rings* (New York, NY: Penguin Group, 2013), p. 88.

2. Phil Jackson and Charley Rosen, *More Than a Game* (New York, NY: Seven Stories Press, 2001), p. 52.

3. Jackson and Rosen, *More Than a Game*, p. 55.

4. Phil Jackson and Hugh Delehanty, *Eleven Rings: The Soul of Success* (New York, NY: The Penguin Press, 2013), p. 60.

5. Phil Jackson and Charley Rosen, *Sacred Hoops* (New York, NY: Hyperion, 1995), p. 129.

6. Richmond, p 101.

7. Jackson and Rosen, *More Than a Game*, p. 77.

8. Richmond, p. 125.

9. Richmond, p. 135.

10. Richmond, p. 138.

11. Richmond, p. 145.

12. Ibid.

13. Roland Lazenby, *Mindgames: Phil Jackson's Long Strange Journey* (New York, NY: Contemporary Books, 2001), p. 155.

CHAPTER 4. COULD THE "BAD BOYS" BE BEATEN?

1. Phil Jackson and Hugh Delehanty, *Eleven Rings: The Soul of Success* (New York, NY: The Penguin Press, 2013), p. 82.

2. Phil Jackson and Charley Rosen, *Sacred Hoops* (New York, NY: Hyperion, 1995), p. 75.

3. Jackson and Rosen, *Sacred Hoops*, p. 172.

4. Jackson and Delehanty, p. 83.

5. Jackson and Rosen, *Sacred Hoops*, p. 102.

6. Jackson and Delehanty, p. 98.

7. Rich Telander, "Da Stadium," *Sports Illustrated*, June 1, 1992, https://www.si.com/vault/1992/06/01/126588/da-stadium-chicago-stadium-home-of-da-bulls-and-da-blackhawks-is-a-glorious-old-sports-palace-in-the-midst-of-a-badly-decayed-neighborhood.

8. Peter Richmond, *Lord of the Rings* (New York, NY: Penguin Group, 2013), p. 166.

9. Jackson and Rosen, *Sacred Hoops*, p. 12.

10. Jackson and Rosen, *Sacred Hoops*, p. 119.

11. Jackson and Rosen, *Sacred Hoops*, p. 116.

12. Jackson and Rosen, *Sacred Hoops*, p. 144.

13. Jackson and Delehanty, p. 84.

14. Jackson and Delehanty, p. 103.

15. Jackson and Rosen, *Sacred Hoops*, p. 103.

CHAPTER 5. BIRTH OF A DYNASTY

1. Phil Jackson and Charley Rosen, *Sacred Hoops* (New York, NY: Hyperion, 1995), p. 6.
2. Phil Jackson and Hugh Delehanty, *Eleven Rings: The Soul of Success* (New York, NY: The Penguin Press, 2013), p. 110.
3. Jackson and Rosen, *Sacred Hoops,* p. 179.
4. Roland Lazenby, *Mindgames: Phil Jackson's Long Strange Journey* (New York, NY: Contemporary Books, 2001), p. 266.
5. Jackson and Delehanty, p. 91.
6. Jackson and Delehanty, p. 114.
7. Jackson and Delehanty, p. 114.
8. Lazenby, p. 169.
9. Lazenby, p. 169.
10. Jackson and Rosen, *Sacred Hoops,* p. 4.
11. David Aldridge, "Oral History: The Life and Times of Commissioner David Stern," NBA.com, Jan 27, 2014, http://www.nba.com/2014/news/features/david_aldridge/01/27/life-and-times-of-david-stern-oral-history-by-david-aldridge/.
12. Jackson and Rosen, *Sacred Hoops,* p. 167.

CHAPTER 6. AN EARLY END TO AN ERA

1. Phil Jackson and Hugh Delehanty, *Eleven Rings: The Soul of Success* (New York, NY: The Penguin Press, 2013), p. 122.
2. Jackson and Delehanty, p. 127.
3. Phil Jackson and Charley Rosen, *Sacred Hoops* (New York, NY: Hyperion, 1995), p. 100.
4. Roland Lazenby, *Mindgames: Phil Jackson's Long Strange Journey* (New York, NY: Contemporary Books, 2001), p. 175.

5. Jackson and Delehanty, p. 130.

6. Jackson and Rosen, *Sacred Hoops*, p. 168.

7. Lazenby, p. 179.

8. Staff, "Michael Jordan Playing Baseball," *Sports Illustrated*, February 15, 2013, https://www.si.com/nba/photos/2013/02/15michael-jordan-playing-baseball#10.

9. Jackson and Delehanty, p. 131.

10. Jackson and Rosen, *Sacred Hoops*, p. 180.

11. Jackson and Delehanty, p. 131.

12. Jackson and Delehanty, p. 133.

13. Jackson and Rosen, *Sacred Hoops*, p. 181.

14. Lazenby, p. 185.

CHAPTER 7. LIFE WITHOUT MIKE

1. Phil Jackson and Charley Rosen, *Sacred Hoops* (New York, NY: Hyperion, 1995), p. 186.

2. Jackson and Rosen, *Sacred Hoops*, p. 137.

3. Phil Jackson and Hugh Delehanty, *Eleven Rings: The Soul of Success* (New York, NY: The Penguin Press, 2013), p. 139.

4. Jackson and Rosen, *Sacred Hoops*, p. 188.

5. Brad Taningco, "Steve Kerr Credits Phil Jackson for His Playing Time Philosophy," Clutchpoints.com, November 14, 2017, https://clutchpoints.com/warriors-news-steve-kerr-credits-phil-jackson-philosophy.

6. Jackson and Delehanty, p. 138.

7. Roland Lazenby, *Mindgames: Phil Jackson's Long Strange Journey* (New York, NY: Contemporary Books, 2001), p. 186.

8. Lazenby, p. 188.

9. Jackson and Rosen, *Sacred Hoops*, p. 190.

10. Jackson and Rosen, *Sacred Hoops*, p. 191.

11. Jackson and Delehanty, p. 141.

12. Jackson and Rosen, *Sacred Hoops*, p. 192.

13. Lazenby, p. 189.

14. Jackson and Delehanty, p. 142.

15. Ibid.

16. Jackson and Rosen, *Sacred Hoops*, p. 194.

17. Jackson and Rosen, *Sacred Hoops*, p. 195.

18. Peter Richmond, *Lord of the Rings* (New York, NY: Penguin Group, 2013), p. 192.

19. Jackson and Rosen, *Sacred Hoops*, p. 20.

20. Richmond, p. 193.

21. Daniel Ginn, "This Mindfulness Teacher Gets Results (just ask Kobe)," *Boston Globe*, May 27, 2015, https://www.bostonglobe.com/maga-zine/2015/05/27/this-mindfulness-teacher-gets-results-just-ask-kobe/mMYGHRJSziVp4DLq2gAzcJ/story.html.

22. Lazenby, p. 204.

23. Jackson and Rosen, *Sacred Hoops*, p. 199.

24. Jackson and Rosen, *Sacred Hoops*, p. 197.

25. Jackson and Rosen, *Sacred Hoops*, p. 199.

26. Jackson and Delehanty, p. 148.

CHAPTER 8. BUILDING A BETTER BULLS TEAM

1. Phil Jackson and Charley Rosen, *Sacred Hoops* (New York, NY: Hyperion, 1995), p. 207.

2. Jackson and Rosen, *Sacred Hoops*, p. 211.

3. Jackson and Rosen, *Sacred Hoops*, p. xvi.

4. Roland Lazenby, *Mindgames: Phil Jackson's Long Strange Journey* (New York, NY: Contemporary Books, 2001), p. 215.

5. Phil Jackson and Hugh Delehanty, *Eleven Rings: The Soul of Success* (New York, NY: The Penguin Press, 2013), p. 156.

6. Jackson and Delehanty, p. 172.

7. Lazenby, p. 245.

8. Ibid.

9. Lazenby, p. 321.

10. Lazenby, p. 383.

11. Lazenby, p. 257.

12. Lazenby, p. 259.

13. Lazenby, p. 264.

14. Jackson and Delehanty, p. 182.

CHAPTER 9. FAREWELLS AND GREETINGS

1. Phil Jackson and Hugh Delehanty, *Eleven Rings: The Soul of Success* (New York, NY: The Penguin Press, 2013), p. 188.

2. Jackson and Delehanty, p. 192.

3. Jackson and Delehanty, p. 195.

4. Phil Jackson and Charley Rosen, *Sacred Hoops* (New York, NY: Hyperion, 1995), p. 25.

5. Jackson and Delehanty, p. 199.

6. Jackson and Delehanty, p. 158.

7. Jackson and Delehanty, p. 150.

8. Jackson and Delehanty, p. 362.

9. Phil Jackson and Charley Rosen, *More Than a Game* (New York, NY: Seven Stories Press, 2001), p. 281.

10. Jackson and Delehanty, p. 203.

11. Jackson and Delehanty, p. 212.

12. Jackson and Rosen, *More Than a Game,* p. 279.

13. Jackson and Delehanty, p. 221.

14. Jackson and Delehanty, p. 218.

15. Roland Lazenby, *Mindgames: Phil Jackson's Long Strange Journey* (New York, NY: Contemporary Books, 2001), p. 371.

16. Jackson and Delehanty, p. 69.

17. Scott Polacek, "Lakers' Jeanie Buss Blames Brother Jim for Breakup with Phil Jackson," Bleacher Report, October 5, 2017, http://bleacherreport.com/articles/2737071-lakers-jeanie-buss-blames-brother-jim-for-breakup-with-phil-jackson.

18. Jackson and Rosen, *Sacred Hoops,* p. 91.

19. Lazenby, p. 367.

20. Lazenby, p. 384.

21. Jackson and Delehanty, p. 226.

22. Jackson and Delehanty, p. 229.

CHAPTER 10. A HOLLYWOOD ENDING

1. Phil Jackson and Hugh Delehanty, *Eleven Rings: The Soul of Success* (New York, NY: The Penguin Press, 2013), p. 233.

2. Jackson and Delehanty, p. 234.

3. Jackson and Delehanty, p. 237.

4. Jackson and Delehanty, p. 246.

5. Jackson and Delehanty, p. 252.

6. Jackson and Delehanty, p. 258.

7. Jackson and Delehanty, p. 252.

8. Jackson and Delehanty, p. 259.

9. Phil Jackson and Charley Rosen, *Sacred Hoops* (New York, NY: Hyperion, 1995), p. x.

10. Jackson and Delehanty, p. 268–269.

11. Jackson and Delehanty, p. 276.

12. Peter Richmond, *Lord of the Rings* (New York, NY: Penguin Group, 2013), p. 267.

13. Richmond, p. 270.

14. Jackson and Rosen, *Sacred Hoops,* p. xii.

15. Jackson and Delehanty, p. 287.

16. Jackson and Delehanty, p. 296.

17. Jackson and Delehanty, p. 300.

18. Jackson and Delehanty, p. 301.

19. Jackson and Delehanty, p. 309.

20. Jackson and Delehanty, p. 302.

21. Jackson and Delehanty, p. 308.

22. Jackson and Delehanty, p. 321.

23. Jackson and Delehanty, p. 327.

24. Richmond, p. 320–325.

25. Jackson and Rosen, *Sacred Hoops,* p. 7.

GLOSSARY

benchwarmer Slang for a member of the team who does not receive much playing time.

buzzer beater A shot taken before the clock expires that goes in after the buzzer signals the end of the shot clock, quarter, half, or game.

fade-away jump shot A shot taken as the shooter leans backward, making it more difficult to block.

fast break Usually occurs after a missed shot, when the rebounding (defensive) team advances the ball upcourt as quickly as possible, hoping to score before their opponents can set up their defense.

field goal A basket scored on any shot other than a free throw. Worth either two or three points, depending on the distance of the attempt.

full-court press When the defense applies pressure to the offense the entire length of the court, before and after the inbound pass.

journeyman A player who has spent short periods of time on several different teams.

pick and roll An offensive play in which a player sets a screen (the pick) for a teammate handling the ball, then moves (rolls) toward the basket to receive a pass.

point guard The position generally responsible for running the offense and distributing the ball to teammates on the offensive side of the court.

put-backs When an offensive player rebounds a teammate's missed shot and immediately makes a basket.

rebound The statistic associated with securing a missed shot after the ball hits the rim of the basket.

roster The list of players on a team and available to play in a game.

screen The ballhandler's teammate assumes a stationary position so the ballhandler's defender runs into the screening player, disrupting the defense.

sixth man A top reserve, generally the first player to enter the game after one of the five starters goes to the bench for a rest.

swingman A player who can play both guard and forward.

transition The phase of the game when Team A misses a shot that is rebounded by Team B, who attempts a fast break.

Triangle offense A strategy popularized by coach Tex Winter that forms a triangle shape through the spacing of players on the floor and passes the ball from point to point in order to obtain an easy shot.

triple double Achieved when a player totals ten or more of three different statistics, such as points, rebounds, and assists.

turnover When a player loses possession of the ball to the other team.

walk-on A college player not offered a scholarship who made his team after a tryout.

FURTHER READING

BOOKS

Jackson, Phil and Hugh Delanty. *Eleven Rings: The Soul of Success*. New York, NY: Penguin Press, 2013.

Jackson, Phil and Hugh Delanty. *Sacred Hoops: Spiritual Lessons of a Hardwood Warrior*. New York, NY: Hyperion, 1995.

Lazemby, Roland. *Michael Jordan: The Life*. New York, NY: Little, Brown and Company, 2014.

WEBSITE

The Mindful Athlete

mindfulathlete.org

The official site of mindfulness teacher George Mumford, whom Jackson brought in to help the team find "flow" in the early 90s.

FILMS

When the Garden Was Eden. ESPN, 2014.

Kobe Doin' Work. ESPN, 2009.

INDEX
